T0149593

LETTERS
TO MY
CHILDREN

PLAYING HIDE AND
SEEK WITH GOD

JILL KATHLEEN BANGERTER

BALBOA.
PRESS

A DIVISION OF HAY HOUSE

Scripture taken from the King James Version of the Bible.

Balboa Press books may be ordered through booksellers or by contacting:

Balboa Press
A Division of Hay House
1663 Liberty Drive
Bloomington, IN 47403
www.balboapress.com
1 (877) 407-4847

Because of the dynamic nature of the Internet, any web addresses or links contained in this book may have changed since publication and may no longer be valid. The views expressed in this work are solely those of the author and do not necessarily reflect the views of the publisher, and the publisher hereby disclaims any responsibility for them.

The author of this book does not dispense medical advice or prescribe the use of any technique as a form of treatment for physical, emotional, or medical problems without the advice of a physician, either directly or indirectly. The intent of the author is only to offer information of a general nature to help you in your quest for emotional and spiritual well-being. In the event you use any of the information in this book for yourself, which is your constitutional right, the author and the publisher assume no responsibility for your actions.

Print information available on the last page.

ISBN: 978-1-5043-7400-2 (sc)
ISBN: 978-1-5043-7401-9 (hc)
ISBN: 978-1-5043-7412-5 (e)

Library of Congress Control Number: 2017901405

Balboa Press rev. date: 02/07/2017

For Chuck, my truest love:
you're the only person who believed in me, encouraged
me, and knew I could write this.
Thank you.

For Matt, Becky and Debbie:
you're the reasons I wrote this.

For my angelic guides: I am so grateful for your
presence. Whenever I asked for your help, you were
there, and I'm eternally grateful to all of you.

To my kids' life partners, Tina, Ken and Steve, and
to all ten of my beautiful grandchildren:
(Zach, Steve, Jeff, Evan, Wyatt, Julia, Jessica,
Lauren, Morgan and Melanie)
let this be my legacy to you, written with all of my
love and gratitude that you're in my life.

CONTENTS

FOREWORD

To Matt, Becky, and Debbie, their life partners, my ten grandkids, and to all my former students whose lives have impacted me…

I'm writing this for lots of reasons, the first one and probably the most important being that my love for all of you has made my life so awesome that I wanted to leave some type of legacy for you. I feel like I failed you in not helping you in starting your own search for God years ago, but I also want to help teen readers, many of whom I've been teaching for the past thirty-five years, to find their way spiritually. I haven't really been totally free to answer your questions or debate religion when you've wanted or needed to.

With this book, I want to tell you about my own spiritual journey and address questions you've had these many years in hope that, perhaps, it will help you on your way. I'm not an infallible prophet, and it's always up to you to accept or reject what I have to say in these pages. If anyone ever tells you how to think, remember that you have enough intelligence and intuition to draw your own conclusions. God gave us free will, after all, and no one has the right to take this away from you. Remember that there are hundreds of paths back to our source. This includes mainstream churches, many of whom may feel threatened by my words and claim that the devil is making me do it! Nonsense. I'm saying only that my reality is what I'm going to write, and that while it makes a great deal of sense for me, I won't be hurt or offended if you disagree with these writings. Maybe they will help you make sense of this world and religion as well.

I believe that everyone must find his or her own spiritual path, and there are many. That's why there've been so many different churches and religions from the beginning of time until the present. People are so different that many different churches are needed. The God I believe in doesn't condemn someone for not belonging to the right church, nor does He send any of His children to "hell" for doing something He doesn't like. What parent do you know will tell his child he's free to do whatever he wants and then turns around and punishes him for doing just that? If a parent does this, I wouldn't consider this person to be a parental role model!

I'm writing this to all of you: my kids, my grandchildren, and to all of my students, past and future. I've been so blessed by your lives and by my contact with you that I want to give something back to all of you. I've been overwhelmed with the joy that all of you have given me and hope that I can return this joy with the light of knowledge and truth as I have come to know it. I feel confident in my spiritual convictions, and I pray that God is guiding me in this endeavor and that it will help each of you who is looking for a way back to our real home and our Father. The more people on Earth who find their way back to God, the more peace and joy we will all experience.

Finally, and most important, to Chuck, my husband, my life, my love: This is also for you. Because of you, I have felt loved and understood in a world that would otherwise have been hostile, lonely and difficult for me. You've been such a treasure all these years that I can never tell you with words how much you have meant to me. I hope you, too, will read this and that, maybe, it will give something to you as well. If it does, it would only be a fraction of what you've given me.

Because of all of you, my life has been extremely rich and rewarding, and I hope this will return some of what you all have given me.

With all of my love always,
Jill, Mom, Grandma, Mrs. B.

How It Began…

INTRODUCTION

When I was a kid, I wanted a puppy for Christmas, talked to God, and there was a puppy. Another time, I lost a stuffed animal that was very valuable to me. I talked to God about it, and it showed up. Things like this often happened to me. Each time it did, my belief in God grew. Jesus told us that if you have the faith of a mustard seed, you can move mountains. While I wasn't exactly moving mountains, I received direct, physical answers to my prayers, and I believed that was just how life worked. Once, my sister Cindy and I were building a "house" outside to play in, and a huge rock that was crucial to the foundation was slowing our progress. Cindy tried and tried but couldn't lift it to put into our "wall." I knew that I could move this huge rock if I asked for help, and I did. Then I walked over, picked it up, and put it in place. I remember Cindy looking at me shocked and asking me how I did that. I told her I had asked for help and then just did it. When we're connected to God, nothing can keep us from accomplishing our dreams, however large or small they are.

We weren't really church goers at our home because my parents had had a bad experience with the Catholic Church when they were married. Sometimes our neighbor would take Cindy and me to the local Methodist church, and other times, our grandparents would take us to their Catholic church. We had both been baptized Catholics, and I believe that's why both my sister and I have been pulled back to the church. The sacraments and the metaphysics behind them are much more than just ritual, but I'll talk about that in a later chapter.

I really began to be drawn to the Catholic Church during my teen years. At this time, I began to voraciously read everything I could get my hands on about Catholicism, spirituality, and the other side of the veil. I remember reading about Lourdes and the life of Saint Bernadette and thinking it was the most beautiful story I had ever read. I also noticed how sensitive I had become to my world and the people in it. This sensitivity made it difficult for me to deal with a tough family, an enormous high school, and the crowds within.

I prayed and was able to manifest objects as a youngster, but it was during my high school years that I had my first vision. This vision helped propel me further on the path to mysticism and metaphysics. I was at Mass with my grandparents and, during one of the prayers, I looked above the altar and saw a beautiful golden orb glowing so brightly I didn't know what it was. I was filled simultaneously with an incredible peace and an overpowering feeling of love that stayed with me for a very long time after the experience. I couldn't understand why other people in the congregation didn't see what I had seen. I never stopped thinking about the experience, but because of my lack of knowledge, I didn't really know what had happened. It wasn't until many years later that I realized it had been a mystical experience.

My college years were years of searching for belonging within a church group. At Ohio University, I became involved with Inter-Varsity Christian Fellowship and sang in the Methodist church choir. I was deeply moved singing The Halleluiah Chorus and continued digging into spirituality and religion. This group, however, didn't approve of anything above and beyond conservative, traditional Methodist teachings. I began to protect my beliefs with my silence, feeling horribly guilty that something was wrong with me because I could just not easily accept what this church group tried to get me to believe. According to them, money, sex and having fun are all evil, and if you feel joy, something is very wrong because you are a sinner. There is nothing joyful about sinners. I couldn't accept this, so my guilt feelings grew, and I became extremely unhappy at Ohio University.

During the 1968-1969 upheavals on college campuses, Ohio University grew threatening for students not into the radical culture, and I decided to transfer to Bowling Green University, a much more politically conservative campus at the time. Spring quarter of 1969, I transferred and soon became involved with Campus Crusade for Christ. This was another step in my search for God. At the same time, I met Chuck.

Campus Crusade had as its members some very spiritual seekers who, I believe, were sincere in loving God. They were, however, fanatical, and I don't believe that any type of fanaticism is good. However, because I naively trusted people, I allowed these Christian crusaders to make me feel even more guilt. I could prove my true Christianity if, according to them, I traveled to Florida during spring break to campaign for Christ by going into bars, standing on tables, and preaching about how Christ could save everyone if they would just allow Him into their lives. I didn't want to do this and, because of my reluctance, was pegged as not being a sincere follower. If I truly had the spirit, they told me, I would do it without question.

At the same time, Chuck and I had grown serious in our relationship, and this same group began telling me that this good man who, incidentally, had attended church his entire life and had been confirmed, was not a true Christian because he refused to get up in front of the Campus Crusade group and proclaim his faith. Obviously, his confirmation in his church didn't count toward this requirement. I was very lucky to have been intuitive at a young age. This "line from

God" kept me from doing stupid things, like going into Florida bars alone and breaking up with a man I deeply loved. When we became engaged, I lost contact with these Crusaders for Christ. At this time in my life, I was already following my "gut feelings."

Since I had no real home church, I joined Chuck's. We married, had you three kids, and began to experience the trials and great rewards of parenting. I was still reading anything I could about metaphysics, spirituality, and the church. One afternoon, I sat down and asked God to show me the answers to my questions. It was a conversation with God just as if I had been sitting across from Him, and I totally expected Him to answer me. The answer, however, didn't come immediately or all at once. This was a life lesson for me. God answers with what is only good for us and what we can handle at the time. Too much knowledge at once would have burned me out or turned me away, or even, perhaps, tipped me into insanity. The knowledge has come as I could handle it and was ready for it: not too soon or too much. When I really needed something, it appeared in some form. Whenever God has had a hand in my affairs and has walloped me with something, it has never failed to blow my mind totally and magnificently.

You might be wondering how I know all that I've written. I've been called hypersensitive, and there's a reason for that. One of the ways God communicates with us is through our feelings. This is called clairsentience, and that's what I am. I'll explain more in subsequent chapters, but suffice it to say that I'm very hypersensitive and feel things in my gut, or around the area of my solar plexus. This is the area in which I feel hostility, love, fear, hurt, and whatever else God is trying to tell me. It's an intense physical feeling and is the reason I've always had stomach problems, even as a child. I pick up things that others don't sense. This trait sometimes causes people to tell me that "I'm being too sensitive," or "Get over it." This has been a burden and is often painful because my feelings are easily hurt, but it's also helped me be a successful teacher over the years. I can sense when a student is troubled or angry and am able to defuse the situation before it blows up. As a result, I've reached some pretty tough students through the years.

This hypersensitivity has also kept me safe. One example of this type of communication occurred when I was in France with my friend, Agnes. We were hiking in the Pyrenees and came up to a stone wall which appeared to be fronting a gently rolling slope. In actuality, there was a sheer cliff right below it. I climbed on the wall to look at the gorgeous view when, suddenly, I was overcome with a crippling fear in my "gut." I quickly climbed down just as Agnes came up to me. Looking over it, she gasped and said she was going to jokingly push me off it, not realizing there was a cliff.

Listening to what God says not only can save our lives, but when we have learned to discern His voice, His communication, which is constant, can make our lives better. I've spent my life working on opening these lines and feel justified in writing about what I know at this point. Although I'm not a medium, nor do I communicate with those on the other side or read auras, as a clairsentient intuitive, I'm qualified to write about what I've discovered through my lifelong studies on my own, through Astara, with the Rosicrucians and with the University of Metaphysics. But this is not an autobiography. It is, rather, an attempt to tell you some of the answers I've gotten over the years to questions you've asked me and how I have gotten these answers. I hope it will help you on your own spiritual quest and perhaps even inspire you to search for other answers of your own. Now that you have kids, be prepared for them to come to you searching. Because we live in a highly technological and materialistic society, it's more crucial than ever to help our young people connect with spirituality and God. Technology is awesome but can get lonely, so I hope this book will help with that.

Note: all citations from the Bible are from the King James Bible.

You've asked me....

HOW DO YOU SEARCH FOR GOD?

CHAPTER 1

When I was a kid, I had the ugliest puppy you can imagine. She had long, gangly legs with white boots, and her coat was a mottled brown with tan and white speckles. I don't remember where we got her, but I named her Bootsie, and she and I became inseparable. I loved that dog.

From day one, Bootsie never had difficulty finding trouble, or it found her, and my dad was unforgiving. Many times we had to run and hide from his wrath when he discovered an overturned garbage can or holes dug in the yard. Maybe our bond was because I was such a loner as a child and felt out of sorts with my family, or maybe we were just kindred spirits searching for love and acceptance. I'll never know. I just know that I loved Bootsie more than anyone or anything else on the planet.

The night Bootsie didn't come home was one of the worst of my young life. I stayed awake all night talking to God, pleading with Him to bring her home to me. He either wasn't listening or just didn't care about my ugly dog because I never saw her again. Dad found her smashed on the road in front of our house and buried her before I could even say good-bye. I can remember looking at the blood stains in the road and crying from the depths of a broken heart, wondering how I would go on living. That night, I just lay on the couch sobbing and crying my eyes out when my dad came into the room and threatened me that, if I didn't stop this nonsensical behavior right then and there, he would take out his strap and beat it out of me. I buried my sobs in the pillow. Although my heart had been shattered, I was too afraid to show it.

The next day, I sat in front of Bootsie's rough grave and just talked to her, crying. I suddenly thought that, maybe, she wasn't really dead after all. I grabbed a stick and began to dig frantically to unearth my friend and companion. After digging a couple of inches, though, someone told me to stop. I still don't know what it was: my conscience, maybe the fear of seeing a lifeless body where my Bootsie had been, or the fear of Dad finding out what I had done. Maybe my guardian angel was sending messages to me to stop. I quit digging and, for some reason, felt my heartache begin to ease. It was like strong arms were hugging and comforting me. I continued with my life, thinking about Bootsie from time to time. This event propelled my curiosity about what was beyond the veil of this physical life.

You were curious about God when you were young and asked where He is, how to find Him, and why we would want to. I had always wondered these things as well. Early in my marriage, I sat down one sunny afternoon and asked God to send me the answers and the knowledge. This is how my quest began. From that time on, things have happened or have appeared to lead me down various paths where I've uncovered spiritual truths. Each answer has led to another pathway that has led to another, and on and on it has gone. Something appears as I'm ready to absorb it.

In our attempts as parents to teach our children, we often have to do so in ways that our kids will understand. Hence, we have stories, myths, poems and many ways to begin to prepare all of you for the immensity of God and His plan. Sometimes people and churches goof, but we all continue to try to guide our kids back to God. Sadly, our attempts sometimes fail miserably and turn kids off toward organized religion.

Some of your favorite fairy tales are disguised views of finding God. Take, for example, *Snow White and the Seven Dwarfs*. This is a story of finding God, the Prince, and awakening to His kingdom. The dwarves symbolize the chakras, and the evil witch is our ego, over which we all need to gain control. In fact, much of the literature I tried to get you to read in my English class were stories about God. Wordsworth's "Intimations of Immortality" and some of the less obvious works allude to life beyond the veil. Many of these writers were enlightened in the sense that they had evolved spiritually to the point of being able to actually witness the Divine.

It's actually inaccurate to talk about searching for God since God is a part of all of us. We don't really need to search, but we do need to reconnect with our one source. It's God's energy and life-force that sustains us and everything in the universe, from rocks and plants to the most evolved and intelligent human. Because His energy is around us and we are in it, when you think about it, nothing really bad can happen to us. I know this sounds like an absurd statement when bad things seem to happen around us all the time. I know people are no doubt going to write me off at this point. It's a cliché to say or hear that we need to trust in God and our cares and worries will be taken care of. I know it's been difficult for me to do this at times as well. However, I have trusted in God during difficult times, and I can honestly say that things have always worked out. The problem is that we often don't see the light at the end of the tunnel. If we remember that we're all on certain paths for a reason, it can become somewhat more bearable when difficulties begin to suffocate us and cause us to lose our way. We often forget to ask for help. Remember that Jesus told us, "Ask and you shall receive." When we are bogged down with problems, we sometimes forget to ask for help.

I've remembered to ask for help during some low periods in my life, and I've never failed to get answers. One example of this was very direct. I had transferred from Ohio University to Bowling Green University in the early seventies for various reasons. After my parents had dropped me off at my dorm during the winter semester, I had no roommate and knew no one. I was scared, lonely and becoming very depressed about the decision I was beginning to regret when I began to cry to God. I told Him how I was feeling and, before I was even finished, my phone rang. It was my cousin Dan calling to take me to dinner.

God answers small as well as large requests. Early in my marriage, I remember when I panicked if I projected our budget and it was even five dollars over. That's how tight our money was, and one day in particular I was scared I would not have money to buy food for Matt. I prayed and went outside into the sunshine. On the sidewalk was a twenty dollar bill. God answers in both direct and indirect ways.

Sometimes God helps us even when we don't ask for it. Do you remember the cliff incident in France I told you about? This was God's intervention and protection without my asking.

Things like this have always happened to me, and I know that I always receive answers to my prayers even if they are not the answers I wanted or expected. Sometimes solutions for a problem just come to me, sometimes objects show up, but God never ignores me. If I lose something that is very valuable to me, I can pray about it, and I'll find it. Doing this requires only a belief and faith in God and aligning yourself to God's purpose.

The title of this chapter, "How Do You Search for God," then, involves beginning to focus on God. You can do this by beginning to meditate daily and to converse just as if He were sitting next to you. The more you meditate, the more you will speed up your vibrations, and the more attuned to Him you will become. There is a bumper sticker that says, "God hasn't moved. You have." This is true of us. God is always with us and around us, but we forget this as we go through our lives in physical matter. If we don't "click" into God's energy, we'll remain oblivious to it and begin to believe we are alone with our troubles.

Try this the next time you're having a problem. Talk to God and tell Him the problem and how it's troubling you. Act as if He is a kindly mother or father figure sitting next to you, and tell Him everything. Lay it on, ask for help, and then stop worrying about it. This is the hard part. Give the worry to God and go about your life without stopping to be scared about the predicament. Keep telling yourself that God is handling it, and let Him. Be sure to watch what happens. Be aware of any answer coming to you, either in the way of thought or inspiration or someone coming into your life who can help. I've even heard an actual voice. It's a physical reality that if you ask, you will receive. What father in his right mind would promise something to his kids and then not follow through? God is the model parent and doesn't do this. He answers, but our problem is that, because He is energy and spiritual and we are physical, we often don't realize He has helped us or answered our prayers when He has, in fact, done so. Nothing is too unimportant for Him to help.

When I was pregnant with Debbie, I got it into my mind that I wanted to crochet an afghan. I bought a beautiful, ornate pattern and multi-colored yarn, came home and sat down to begin. I had knitted a lot and felt it wouldn't be too difficult to transfer that skill to crocheting. Wrong. I couldn't figure out how to do it. I asked all of the experts in the family: Great-Grandma Secunde, your aunts, and anyone else I could think of. I was finally told that perhaps I should begin with an easier pattern. I put it away, thinking it was one of the prettiest patterns

I had seen and went to bed wondering how I could get over this hurdle. That night, I had a crystal clear, psychic dream showing me exactly how to crochet this pattern. When I awakened, I sat down and did it. No one helped me except my dream. Someone on the other side had given me a lesson, and I remembered it consciously and brought it back with me. This incident helped to further convince me of the reality of the world beyond the physical and of the helpers within that world.

Searching for our reconnection to God, then, is basically the same as searching for anything else. You need to figure out what you want to search for and then simply ask for help. Answers might come suddenly, but in my experience, they have also arrived quietly and subtly. Once I was troubled and asked the angels for a sign that they were with me. That day in the mail, I received an angel ornament from Tina. I've had a book fall into my hands, I received something in the mail, I observed something physically in the environment, or I met a teacher who guided me. Once you've asked, you will receive the answers as you can handle them. In fact, this is how I became a member of Astara. One of their angels, and I still don't know who it was, sent me an invitation to study with them. Those studies opened the doors wide to my pursuit of metaphysics.

If you want to truly find and get to know God in your life, all you have to do is ask. You'll begin to find Him. Be prepared, though, not to learn everything all at once. The universe and God are far too enormous and complicated to learn it quickly. It takes a lifetime and then some, and I'm convinced beyond a doubt that this spiritual quest is our purpose for being here: so that we can grow into what we were meant to become as children of Gods. It takes a lot more than just twelve years of learning to do that. Good luck and God-speed in your own searches!

MEDITATION:

Meditation is the truest form of prayer. It is during meditation that we can calm ourselves and listen for God's voice, and in doing this, we can also raise our vibrations so that we can tune ourselves, not unlike a radio station, to God's vibes. The closer we get to this, the more psychic we become and the more we can see, hear, feel or see God's answers. Following each chapter, then, I'll teach you a little about meditation so that you can begin to attune yourselves and grow in God's Energy.

Start by picking a place where you are the least likely to be disturbed, preferably a place you like and feel comfortable in. Soothing music in the background may help you to quiet your thoughts, and you can either sit up straight or lie flat on a comfortable surface. I don't have any luck meditating while reclining because whenever I do, I fall asleep. In fact, sometimes I even fall asleep while meditating sitting upright. You have to find the best position for yourselves.

To start, it's important to quiet your mind. This can be a challenge that you will need to practice. Breathe in and out deeply three times, ask God to be with you, and visualize a warm, sparkling golden light just above your head that comes down to envelope you. Try to feel love. If you can't, it might help to think of someone that you know you love. Grab that feeling to keep with you. Then just keep your mind blank for a few minutes, concentrating on your breaths. If any thoughts come into your mind, push them out and focus on your breathing. This should start you on your path to meditation. Following each chapter, I'll give you more tips to get you into deeper meditations.

You've asked me...

WHO AND WHERE IS GOD ANYWAY, AND WHAT IS OUR RELATIONSHIP TO HIM?

CHAPTER 2

This is a very tough question to answer young children, but by the same token, young kids seem to be more tuned into the universe and all the mystical aspects involved. This is why Jesus told us that "Except ye be converted, and become as little children, ye shall not enter into the kingdom of heaven" (Matthew 18:3). As a young mom, I don't think I had learned and grown enough at that point to really clarify it for you, so I'll try now.

Literature, churches, society, and parents all try to depict God as a benevolent father with a long white beard sitting on a throne above us and answering certain prayers while ignoring others. As finite, physical beings, it's hard to visualize an intelligent, creative being who has no body. Because of our perception that God sometimes doesn't answer us when we pray, we start to rationalize and explain to ourselves why this happens. Maybe it was a selfish request. Maybe we shouldn't have even asked, or maybe it hurts someone else. As a child grows up, then, and becomes more educated, it becomes more and more difficult to believe all the things she has been told while growing up and, unless that child really begins a search on her own, she may begin to feel like all the stories and explanations were children's tales to be discarded as she grows up. Besides, she might ask, how does one man answer everyone's prayers? It's easy to make God a cliché or a symbol and to not accept Him as a reality.

God is not a cliché, nor is He just for children. He's also not a crutch, as some non-believers would try to convince us. He is indeed a reality to be trusted and loved by everyone. God is so real to me that I sit and talk with Him as if He's right there with me. How do I do this, you ask? Sometimes I talk out loud, sometimes I just think the words, and I especially feel the connection when I'm deep in meditation. I know God is listening because of the direct answers to my prayers that I've received.

So back to the question of exactly who is God. Earlier people had images of Him that they depicted in their drawings and literature. Moses saw Him as a burning bush. Michelangelo saw Him as a strong father figure. Cartoons picture him as old and gray, and Jesus told us to pray to "our Father who is in Heaven." So who is He? Please remember that what I'm saying here is what I've come to know from my own searching, prayers and meditations.

Once upon a time, there was a huge void where a great spirit lived who was lonely. This Spirit was all there was and filled the universe like water fills the ocean. If you take a jar and place pebbles in it and then fill it with sand, all the spaces aren't totally filled yet. However, if you take a pitcher of water and pour it into the jar, that water will permeate the sand and pebbles and then fill in all the tiny gaps. The oxygen, however, fills everything, including the water. This is how I picture God's spirit. He's so fine that He can fill in everywhere and anywhere, but He's conscious, intelligent, and made of love energy. This love energy is real and tangible even though we can't see it. This is what God is. Just like you can't see the wind but can feel it and know it's there, so is God. Whenever you feel love, that's God. Love energy is a real and physical manifestation of our creator. If you know this, then you always know He's there even though you can't see Him. It's not just a cliché that God is love. This is what He is. I'll explain more about how we're a part of Him a little later when I talk about our spirit bodies.

But, you've asked, what does God actually look like? No one on the planet has actually seen God except for Jesus, but that doesn't mean He's far away and untouchable. A few years ago, I attended an A.R.E. conference at which, among other activities, we were led in a group meditation in which we were paired up with partners. Touching our hands lightly together, we meditated and, during this meditation, I saw my partner's soul. She appeared as a very light, ethereal, floating body that transcended the physical realm, but she clearly appeared with her face and personality. It was an amazing experience, one that I've never forgotten and that has helped me formulate my picture of God. You see, if we're made in His likeness and image, then my friend's soul must look similar. Since then, during a recent meditation, God's image popped into my vision.

Some people who are visual clairvoyants actually see pictures on the back of their eyelids. While I usually am clairsentient, occasionally I also have very clear images, and in fact, had another awesome experience at this same workshop. Working with a group of about ten strangers, we chanted OM together while holding hands with one member in the center of our group. Our assignment was to go around the group and tell what we saw. I was the first, and when we had done the chant, a clear picture of a nun popped into my vision on the back of my eyelids. Thinking it was my imagination, I almost said I saw nothing, but in keeping with the assignment, I decided to share. The lady in the middle simply nodded and went on to the next person until everyone in the group had stated what they had seen, if anything. She then went around and told us the relevance of our visions. Beginning with me, she told the group that she had been a nun many years ago, blowing my mind.

Because of this experience, when I saw this image of God, I knew He was honoring me with His image, and ever since this vision, my prayers have changed. I now feel that I'm praying to a real and living God. Prior to this, I wasn't certain I could say I knew Him, but now I really feel like I'm praying to our Father in Heaven. In my vision of Him, He appeared as a Golden Orb, very similar to the soul of the lady at the conference except glowing with a golden, sparkling light that was bright like our sun. His face was clearly human and filled with love, and the golden light energy surrounding His face in the orb radiated outward to the universe, encompassing everything with this living force and shimmering with sparkling, golden light. I imagine God to be too blinding for us to behold since, in my vision, He radiated golden light, but His form was all-powerful and all-loving. I felt as if loving arms were hugging me while this vision lasted.

If you're thinking that love is just a feeling and really isn't real, think again. Love is the most powerful force in our world, and it comes from God. Love can make you sweat and pass out, it can keep you awake at night and make you lose weight, it can change people, and it can stop wars. Even the most powerful weapons we have can't always do that. If love is only a thought or emotion, it wouldn't have the power to do all that, so if God is this love energy, you can imagine how powerful He is just by thinking of what love can do.

If God is energy and love, it might be easy for you to think of Him like we think of a lightning bold: an energy that is just energy and has no thoughts or feelings or consciousness, but God isn't a lightning bolt. God is intelligent and conscious and has feelings, and now I know He also has a form. Again, I can guess this because we're told that we are "made in His image," and when children are made in the image of their parents, they have many of the same traits. Because we love and weep and feel and laugh, and because we take after God, I can only assume that God also loves and weeps and feels and laughs as well. This is easy to forget since we tend to put God on a pedestal and think of Him as being far, far removed from us as humans, but He's not far away. In fact, He's all around us and in us as well. We've just managed to block Him out.

Evan, you've wondered who made God if God made all of us. I can't honestly answer this question other than to say that, because God is infinite and has always been and always will be, no one made Him. God is the source of the energy in the universe. Because God is infinite, as His children, so are we infinite. Children are like their parents, as you know, so if God is infinite, we have to be as well. In fact, as children of God, we are actually future Gods, or Gods in the making. That's why we're going through all the stuff we're experiencing: so we can learn to be good Gods. Where do you think this puts the belief that we are horrible, dirty, rotten sinners and have no business even looking for God? As children of God and, ergo, future Gods, how can we possibly be horrible, dirty, rotten sinners with no business communicating with our Father? When kids misbehave, does that make them evil? This belief was perpetuated over the ages by churches to control people and has done incredible damage to our psyches, often blocking our movement closer to our true source. We can't connect with God if we constantly feel guilty.

God appeared to me as a Golden Orb with a loving face shining out on His creations. His aura is a golden energy that permeates everything: rocks, ground, water, plants, animals and people. This energy swirls around, is inside us and outside us and keeps everything moving along and living. Various spiritual disciplines have called this energy prana or chi or the Holy Spirit, and as the finest vibration in the universe, every living being and creation has it inside them. Our good feelings come from this energy, and this is undoubtedly where we got the saying that God is love. If you are feeling love and joy, you're feeling God because love and joy are synonymous with God. If you are feeling hate or fear or another emotion, you're distracted by life and have blocked your connection to God. This is when people commit evil acts and become wicked. They are still, however, God's kids and still future Gods. Sometimes we feel better when we peg people as low-lives and "bad" because it makes us feel superior and, thus, good about ourselves. The fact is, though, that God loves us all regardless of the mistakes we make. It doesn't matter whether we think of ourselves as the "bad guys" or the "good guys."

This is a very simplistic explanation of what I know of God. If you keep searching, you will discover how much more there is to learn, and it's never-ending. I don't think I'm ever going to know it all, but every little tidbit of knowledge I gain makes me thirsty for more, so I'll keep on trying to learn it until I return to my spiritual home once again.

MEDITATION:

Start out as instructed in the last chapter. In your chosen quiet place, sit for a moment and breathe deeply, trying to clear your head of all vagrant thoughts that pop into it. Continue breathing and focusing on your breath, ask for God to be with you, and visualize a golden orb just above your head. Focus on this picture for a few moments, and then picture this orb moving down like a giant bubble and enveloping you in its warmth. Feel love surrounding you and inside you. If an errant thought pops up, push it back and continue focusing on this golden orb. Keep your mind blank and just imagine this orb with a healing, loving presence that permeates every cell of your being. Remain still and focused on this orb for as long as you can until you return to the present.

You've asked me…

WHO ARE WE REALLY, AND WHY ARE WE HERE?

CHAPTER 3

I'll go back to my statement that God has feelings and was alone. He wanted companionship, so He began to create beings in His image, and that would be us. We were originally born in spirit on the other side of the veil, or in the spiritual realm, but that doesn't mean that we were less conscious or less loving or less human than we are now. Paul writes in Romans 8:16-17 that … "we are the children of God: And if children, then heirs; heirs of God, and joint-heirs with Christ…" (Holy Bible). When God created us, we had spirit bodies but, as God's children, just like our own children, we needed to learn and grow and, thus, go to school. Guess what school is? It's your physical existence here on Earth, and that's what your purpose is: to learn how to grow and become like your Father. You do this by experiencing physical existence and all the trials and tribulations this experience brings. You are gods-in-the-making!

God gave you free will. That means that you made the decision to incarnate but, as children, you obviously needed guidance on what lessons to go for in this life. You all have spirit guardians on the other side, and these guardians helped you on the spiritual plane to map out your lives. You chose your parents and where you would live and what trials and challenges you would undergo, all to help you on your paths of becoming like your Father. That's where the free will comes in. You decided what lessons to learn and how to go about it, so you can all stop blaming your parents for your problems now. You chose them!

Let me explain a little about our bodies. Within our spiritual bodies is our life force. It's the part of God's energy that is within us. Our soul connects us to God and our physical bodies, and this soul is filled with God's energy. However, because we are in the physical and sense through our five physical senses, we have forgotten that this finer body is present and don't sense it as well. This is why we sometimes find it difficult to believe in the reality of God. Any search for God should entail working toward union of this energy force within us and a conscious recognition of our connection with God. When we meditate and go "into our closet to pray," as Jesus instructed, we are attempting to commune and become one with God, which is the "atonement," or "at one-ment" with God. We consciously merge with God's energy and become one, which we are anyway but have simply forgotten.

Picture it like this. Close your eyes and imagine a golden bubble surrounding the entire universe. This bubble is God. I had a flash of Him as a brilliant, golden orb with an incredibly loving, intelligent face. Nothing is left out of this bubble, and inside, the bubble is filled with golden love energy. Now picture the bubble constantly moving and creating new little bubbles of all shapes and sizes inside the big one, with all the newer bubbles still filled with that golden light energy. All of the little bubbles are exactly like the big one, and all are filled with the same energy. They're baby bubbles. Now imagine the bubble is God's aura and all the little bubbles are His creations, from the planets to the rocks and plants to animals and people. We are all a part of God and filled with God's energy. This is how I picture God, except the bubble is intelligent, loving and conscious. He is a personal God for all of us, and in fact, we are all also a part of one another. That's hard to swallow, especially when we're confronted with annoying people. The next time you feel the need to criticize someone, remember that God is in that person as much as He is in you, and this includes the brilliant scientist, the nerd at school, even the criminal in prison. He's in your gay neighbor or the gang member in your neighborhood, as well as Catholics, Jews, Muslims, and protestants. We all have the same amount of God's life-force in us. It's just that some of us are less aware of it than others. Because of the free-will that God gave each of us, we're allowed to do good or bad, and the less we know of God's energy within, sometimes the more bad we become. This does not mean that God hates us. It means we have consciously moved away from God, and this is what sin is: disconnect from God. This is not good for us or for our world.

So just how do we take on our physical bodies? Once we make the decision to incarnate, the science is there as to how we materialize. Metaphysics is the science that explains it. The universe and everything in it is made up of vibrations, from super-fast to super-slow. The slower the vibe, the heavier the matter. When the vibrations are the slowest, physical matter is created. Think of the ice cube. In its slowest state, it's rock-hard, but as the vibrations speed up, that rock-hard ice cube becomes the softer water and then the ethereal steam. From steam, water condenses and becomes liquid and then solid when frozen. This is the picture I have of us materializing. Our soul begins to slow down our vibrations, and a part of us begins to take on a physical body within the womb we've chosen. We connect it to us with the proverbial silver cord. This is our "descent" into matter, or "the Fall" of man mentioned in Genesis Chapter 3. To become physical people, we first hovered over our mothers while they were pregnant, and our soul helped to form our baby bodies in her womb. Remember that we choose our parents, and then we reserve that particular womb and body and cause the cells in the embryo to begin to multiply and divide. The baby grows in our mom's stomach, and we finally enter the body at birth, although sometimes the soul can enter a little bit sooner. I felt Matt enter early in my pregnancy. He was anxious to be born, and I felt a quickening before I even knew I was pregnant. I've always thought that the feeling I had was his soul laying claim to his little body, and I even knew he would be a boy at this point.

You might want to call me crazy, but if you think a moment about this process, science has no answer for how the cells "miraculously" know how to begin to divide and form the different organs and grow into a baby. They know it happens and have explained quite a bit about the process, but I've never heard any scientist describe who or what causes all those cells to begin to multiply and divide and become a human other than offering theories of how it happens. Science can only go so far before they have to look to a higher intelligence or power, and that would be God. Since I can't prove this, consider it another theory.

As we become immersed in our physical bodies and the physical world around us, we begin to forget our true selves. If we remembered, we wouldn't want to stay here and tough it out because the beauty of the other side would pull us back. In order to sense and experience the physical world, we develop an ego that interprets the world through our five senses for us and basically keeps us alive. This ego often directly conflicts with what our Soul wishes for us because the ego is concerned only with physical survival. The soul knows there is no death. As we grow older, we tend to shut off the communication between our higher self, or our God-Spark, and begin to look at life only through the ego. Because of this, we lose our connection with God and begin to think we're all alone. Some people become so far removed from their God-Spark that they begin to do evil and become truly "lost" and apart from

God. It's our egos that create all the problems in our world, and we've given this part of us a name: Satan. I'll talk more on this topic later.

The entire universe has many planes of existence. Do you remember reading Jesus's words about many mansions? He said, "In my Father's house are many mansions: if it were not so, I would have told you. I go to prepare a place for you." (John 14:2) Jesus was trying to explain to unscientific people about the many planes of existence, but he does not go into great detail since the people would not have understood.

On the other side where we actually came from, we were in our spirit bodies. These bodies are ethereal and can be moved by thought and feeling. Our bodies are multi-faceted. We have a physical body on the dense physical plane, emotional bodies on the astral or desire plane, and mental bodies on the mental plane. Our spiritual bodies reside on the spiritual plane. Our bodies together resemble an egg that surrounds and penetrates our physical bodies and extends a little beyond what we experience through our five senses. Some people can see these other bodies of ours as auras. These are depicted in many paintings of Christ and Mary as golden glows over their heads. If I really focus, I can see some auras. In fact, I often see an aura around the Eucharist in our church. During our last Easter Vigil, I experienced a real miracle which I'll describe in a later chapter. This is how I know we have these different bodies.

The center, or nucleus, of our bodies is the third eye. When it opens through spiritual practices and work, we begin to find the truth and know who we really are and where we came from. The more we work toward opening up this third eye, the more mystical experiences we'll have and the more we'll see of the spiritual plane. Jesus explained this in Matthew 6:22: "The light of the body is the eye; if therefore thine eye be single, thy whole body shall be full of light." In other words, when we manage to open up our third eye, we will achieve the atonement, or at-one-ment, with God, our Higher Self or God-Spark. Jesus says further in Matthew 6:23: "…if thine eye be evil, thy whole body shall be full of darkness"… or distant from God, shut off and unable to see His Light. These are our real bodies. They are connected to God and are immortal.

While on the "other side," which is where we come from at birth and return to at physical "death," we get together with our spiritual guide and determine what our physical life path will be after we decide to take on our physical body again. I say again because we do this hundreds of times until we have learned and experienced enough of physical matter to help us in our evolution. This is called Reincarnation, and most of the world believes it to be true. Many churches teach otherwise, but you can find mention of it frequently in the Bible. Jesus Himself said, "Truly, truly, I say to you, unless one is born anew, he cannot see the kingdom of God" (John 3:3), and "I say unto thee, Except a man be born of water and of the Spirit, he cannot enter into the kingdom of God" (John 3:5). The water is the amniotic sac in which we float until physical birth. Being born in the spirit is what we call death, or our return to our spiritual body. These verses and many more in the Bible clearly talk of rebirth and reincarnation. Jesus also told the disciples that He is "not of the world" (John 17:14-16), explaining that His true body is a spirit body and not the flesh we experience through our senses.

We are, first and foremost, spiritual bodies living in a physical shell. We make the decision and are drawn back to a certain place and family that will help us learn the physical world's lessons. Perhaps we're lacking something we need to address, and we are attracted to the vibrations of the parents who will be able to provide that "lesson" or "experience." With God's help, we focus and direct ourselves to the situation that will best serve us, connecting to our new bodies via the "silver cord," a spiritual life line or umbilical cord that we have throughout our lives.

It breaks only when we are ready to leave our bodies to return to our real home.

There are many "layers" or levels to our bodies, and the vibrations range from quick to slow. As I stated previously, our physical bodies are the slowest vibration, and we sense the world through our five physical senses. A slightly "quicker" body of ours is the desire body, and this is the body which experiences the feelings of desire. Moving up the range to faster vibes is the mental body, and finally we also have our spirit body. All of these bodies are entwined together. Again, picture it like an egg with our spirit body the egg white that extends beyond our physical body but permeates through it. The yolk is at the center and represents the physical body. All of these bodies belong to us as individuals and are connected to God. This is similar to how electrons, protons and neutrons revolve around their nucleus within molecules and how the planets in our solar system revolve around the suns. Everything is in constant motion.

We operate on seven-year cycles and do not really experience total soul habitation of our physical bodies until we are in our twenties. Puberty is characterized by emotions because we have not yet experienced the full descent into physical matter by our spirit bodies, and this is why the teen years can be so difficult.

How do I know all this? As I've previously written, God talks to us through many means: intuition, directly, through feelings, and through other people or teachers who are spiritually advanced enough to actually consciously travel to the other side "out of their bodies" and bring back this information. There are lots of such people helping us on our way. Prayer and meditation help us to speed up our bodies' vibrations, and the more we speed up these vibrations, the more we see, hear and feel the other side. I have always been intuitive, but the more I study metaphysics and the more consistently I meditate, the more attuned

I become to God and my spiritual self, and the more I grasp. I weed out those bits of information that I just cannot accept and retain the rest as factual knowledge. You need to do the same and figure things out for yourselves. That's why Jesus spoke in parables. It was what the people could understand and accept in that day and age. You'll hear and understand as you are able to as well, just as Jesus said: "He that hath ears to hear, let him hear" (Matthew 4:9).

MEDITATION:

Begin as before. Sit or recline in your quiet place, and inhale and exhale several times. Empty your mind of any thoughts and ask God to be present with you and to guide you. Visualize the golden orb above your head and then moving down to engulf your entire being in warmth and love. Visualize this golden light permeating every cell of your being, filling you with peace and love, and allow yourself to just sink into its peace. Inside your head, focus on the area of the third eye and relax into the darkness or the swirling colors. Maintain this for as long as you can, just experiencing what comes to you. Come back to your reality when you're ready.

You've asked me...

HOW ARE WE CONNECTED TO THE UNIVERSE?

CHAPTER 4

When I was a child, I discovered a private cave in a wooded lot that I was sure no one else knew about. This cave was essentially a brush pile that had a hole large enough for me to crawl into, but when I was inside, I felt sheltered from the problems of my world. I stayed there for what seemed like hours, alone, reading and sometimes just thinking. I can remember imagining us as ants with giant people hovering over us who we couldn't see in our smallness. I wondered whether it kept going and going like that.

I was unfamiliar with Hermetics at the time, but the expression, "As above, so below," according to the Hermetic axiom, can help to explain the workings of the universe in a very simplistic way that somewhat parallels my childhood ponderings. We all know that we have a sun in our universe with planets that revolve around it. This is a fact that has obviously been proven by science. We also know for a fact that everything in the universe is made up of molecules that consist of electrons, protons and neutrons that revolve around a nucleus. A number of factors determine what these molecules form, but this is a topic I won't try to delve into as a non-scientist. I'll leave that to the people who have spent their lives studying these topics.

Our bodies also revolve around a "nucleus." Our different bodies, which consist of the physical, astral, mental and spiritual, surround and permeate us and are centered in the third eye, which could be compared to a molecular "nucleus." It's easy to compare the heavenly bodies orbiting the sun with our bodies on the different planes "orbiting" around our third eye. Each cell in our body also has electrons, protons and neutrons that revolve around a nucleus. And so it goes, "As above, so below."

Since then, my studies and meditations have led me to understand the universe as much more. One plane of existence consists of the spiritual realm where the vibrations and molecules are the finest and permeate everything. This is the God energy, also called prana or chi in different spiritual traditions. I think of it as God's aura. This energy is the creative force in the universe and gets the ball rolling for everything in existence. This energy, as previously stated in my description of the different bodies that make up our aura, is everywhere, filling in all the spaces and cracks between, among, and in molecules, including ourselves. This is the Holy Spirit, the Comforter that Jesus asked God to send us. He is inside and around all of us. This includes our animal and plant friends as well, and this is why Jesus tells us, in John 14:16, 17: "And I will pray the Father, and he shall give you another Comforter, that he may abide with you forever; Even the Spirit of truth; whom the world cannot receive, because it seeth him not, neither knoweth him: but ye know him; for he dwelleth with you, and shall be in you." He's referring to the Holy Spirit, and this is why we're all brothers and sisters. God is in each of us.

As I previously stated, there are four major planes of existence: the spiritual, the mental, the astral and the physical. These planes all interconnect with one another with no line of demarcation where one begins and the other ends. These planes of existence are also within us. Our dense bodies are obviously the physical plane. Our desires and emotions are on the astral plane, our thoughts are on the mental plane, and our intuition, will, imagination and spirit abide on the spirit plane. The physical world embodies our vital and dense body, and this is where plants, minerals, animals and people abide, living, breathing, and experiencing the physical world through our senses, which are controlled by our ego. When we begin to experience emotions and desires, we move into our desire or astral bodies. This plane can be seen by psychics as swirling colors in our aura. Our thoughts and mental activities also swirl in our auras within our mental bodies, or the world of thought, and once we have a thought, it remains in this world as an actual thing. This is what is meant when spiritual teachers warn us that thoughts are things. Thoughts can be incredibly powerful, strong enough to build sky scrapers. Will and imagination reside in the spirit world, and this world is also visible in our auras to those who can see them. In fact, early paintings depict these auras as halos, so people have been aware of auras since ancient times.

We have seven energy centers within our bodies called chakras, and these energy bodies act like the currents in the oceans, generating energy and motion. If you remember from your art classes the colors on the art wheel as Roy G Biv, think of the chakras as radiating the same colors. The base or root chakra is like a wheel spinning red and is located at the base of the spine. This chakra pulls energy up from the earth and disseminates it to the rest of the body, but when it's blocked, it can create blocks to the rest of the energy centers moving up our bodies. This chakra connects us to the physical world and regulates basic survival instincts. If we experience a traumatic situation in our early childhood, this chakra could be blocked, leading to a later feeling of being a victim and uncertain of our safety and physical existence.

The next energy center, or sacral chakra, is located around the area of the ovaries in women or the testes in men and spins orange when it's clear. It controls our physical health and well-being as well as our sexuality and feelings of pleasure and abundance. It pulls in and regulates energy from the desire/astral/emotional world, and it's the means for giving and receiving sexual pleasure. A block at this chakra could be caused by illness or an abusive situation and can create a feeling of martyrdom where an individual feels the need for depriving himself of happiness and pleasure.

The third chakra, the solar plexus chakra, is located slightly below the area of the navel and spins yellow, connecting us to the mental plane. This is where we experience "gut" feelings, fear and will. This is where the ego abides and where our feelings of self-worth and identity come from. If blocked, we experience low self-esteem and have a difficult time in securing self-confidence. A person with a blocked solar plexus chakra is one who must build herself up by pulling others down because of a low self-image. They're the people pleasers who feel that they must bend to the will of others to feel any self-importance.

The fourth chakra, the heart chakra, spins green and is the center for feeling, especially love. It bridges the astral and mental planes and is our love-center. We all know what a broken heart feels like, and this is one way this chakra can become blocked. If a person's heart chakra is blocked, she can only love conditionally and might withhold her love if she judges the recipient is not valued enough for an unconditional love. She might find it difficult to find a long-lasting love. In fact, if any one or all of these chakras are blocked, we can become disconnected from our energy source and, if allowed to continue, this disconnection can create both mental and physical illness.

The fifth chakra, the throat chakra, connects us to the spiritual plane and lies near the throat. When this chakra spins free and clear blue, it allows us to speak our truth and act with courage. Living in fear of expressing one's beliefs and hiding one's feelings can block this chakra. One of the effects of a blocked throat chakra is thyroid problems.

The brow chakra connects us to the spiritual plane. When we are ready and have done our spiritual work, it allows us to see clearly with spiritual vision. This chakra spins indigo, and the person who only sees the world intellectually without seeing the spiritual aspect of our world will experience a blockage at this chakra.

Finally, the seventh chakra, which spins a deep violet, pulls spiritual energy down through our crown and into the rest of our body. This is the center for knowing God and reaching unity with the spiritual realm. If a person believes himself to be only a physical being and separate from God and the universe, the crown chakra will be blocked. There are also minor chakras in various parts of our body which I'll save for another time. When any one or more of the chakras are blocked, physical and mental illness can be the result.

Again, think of these energy centers as vortices or currents. They resemble the oceans and their waves of motion. The chakras pull and push waves of energy that come from the various planes of existence down into our bodies. These centers can also be compared to floodgates. Everyone has blocks to these centers that we placed there for our own protection at one time. You may have had a traumatic event in your childhood that would have destroyed you if not for the block, or you may have feelings of guilt or anger that have blocked one or more of the centers to various degrees, sometimes from long ago. If you went through a painful divorce, lost a child or a loved one, or had a brutal argument with someone and you can't rid yourself of the sadness or grief as a result, one or more of your chakras could be blocked. If not eventually cleared, this block can cause more problems in your physical and emotional bodies. This is an entire book topic in itself, and because

I can't cover it in this book, I would recommend seeking help with someone who is an expert in cleansing the chakras and healing all parts of the body, both physical and etheric. It's crucial for your health as well as for your spiritual advancement. The meditation tip that follows is only a basic cleansing of the chakras and may not be sufficient for opening up blockages.

MEDITATION FOR CLEANSING THE CHAKRAS

As usual, sit comfortably with your eyes closed, and visualize the golden bubble over your head moving down to engulf your entire body in warmth. Relax and empty your mind of all thoughts. Breathe in and out seven times. Beginning at the root chakra, visualize the chakra spinning clockwise and red. Affirm to yourself that you are safe and self-sufficient and that you have all you need. As you mentally state this affirmation, see the chakra spinning out the black particles of negativity until it's spinning a vibrant and clear red.

Breathe in and out seven times again. Moving to the sacral chakra, visualize it spinning clockwise a brilliant orange. Affirm to yourself that you appreciate and enjoy your life and the universe's abundance and beauty, and see the chakra spinning out the black spots of negativity until the wheel is clear and brilliantly orange.

Take seven breaths as you move up to the solar plexus chakra, and visualize it spinning yellow. Affirm to yourself that you're a valuable, creative person able to meet the world and everyone in it with confidence and strength. See the chakra spinning clockwise a bright, sparkling yellow, eliminating any negativity and feelings of poor self-image.

Again, breathe in and out seven times as you move up to the heart chakra. Visualize it spinning clockwise a bright and vibrant green while affirming to yourself that you love deeply and are deeply loved. Imagine the chakra spinning out old hurt and betrayal as the green becomes a glowing green wheel. Breathe in and out another seven times as you visualize the throat chakra spinning clock-wise a beautiful blue. Affirm to yourself that you're an awesome communicator who speaks your truth courageously and boldly, and see the chakra spinning any negative, buried emotions or communication. See it spinning out negativity until it spins a deep, brilliant blue.

Breathe in and out seven times while visualizing the brow chakra in the area between your brows, spinning clockwise a heavenly indigo color. Look beyond your intellectualism and see yourself as a spiritual person clothed in a physical body and see the negative rigidity spin out as this wheel becomes a clear indigo.

Finally, breathe in and out seven times and picture your crown chakra opening up to welcome the universal spirit and become one with God and the cosmos. Let go of any egotism and see this wheel spinning out negativity, becoming clear, vibrant, deep violet.

Relax your breathing, empty your mind, and sit comfortably for as long as you can before gently returning to your physical world.

You've asked me....

HOW AND WHY DO WE PRAY AND MEDITATE, AND HOW IN THE WORLD DOES GOD HEAR ALL OF US?

CHAPTER 5

Jesus said in Mark 11:24: "...I say unto you, What things soever ye desire, when ye pray, believe that ye receive *them,* and ye shall have *them."* When I was a kid, I had a beloved stuffed animal. Actually, I had a ton of them, but this one was particularly important to me. I don't know why. It was one of those kid things, I guess. One day, I couldn't find him anywhere. Mind you, my stuffed animals weren't just toys. They were actual beings that I talked with and tucked into bed at night. I was a strange child. Anyway, I asked God to show me where he was, and I went into a room, and there was my stuffed friend. This happened to me so many times that I just assumed everyone could do it. You can. You've simply forgotten. All these years later, as a Grandma, I still pray when I lose something important, and there it will be. The power here is belief. I have always believed that if something is important enough to me to pray to find it, God will manifest it, and He does. Chuck recently lost his wallet in the movies and combed the aisle where he was sitting. As you know, losing a wallet with credit cards, drivers' license and money is no small matter nowadays. Needless to say, he was upset. I had been waiting for him in the lobby, and he came out pretty distressed, so in I went. I said a quick but fervent prayer to God to help me find it, and I went to the row where we were sitting. There it was, in plain view, slightly tucked under the arm of the chair. He should have seen it there but didn't. I believe God manifested it for us. Prayer is as real as talking on the phone or sending text messages.

I often marvel that people feel they can't believe in God or prayer simply because they are unable to see Him or feel Him and hear an actual auditory response, yet these same people think nothing of receiving movies and sending messages and photos over the air waves without a thought or question. We may not "hear" a voice when we pray or "see" God, but prayer is every bit as real and effective as any of the technology that God has allowed us to "invent" or "discover."

We ask by praying, but how many times have we prayed fervently for something that just did not come to pass? Why does God promise us, "Ask and you will receive" but then seems to not follow through? In effect, WHY doesn't God answer our prayers? Why did my dad or aunt or husband die when I asked so desperately for God to save them? When something sad like this happens, it's very easy to blame God for stealing our loved one away, but what if it was up to us to leave when we choose to do so at a soul level? We can only answer for ourselves as to when we're prepared to depart, not for the other person. When my dad had cancer, he bravely endured horrible experimental chemo treatments that extended his life long enough for him to get his affairs in order. During the ordeal, he told me how excited he was to see his own mother soon. I made the statement that yes, that would be good, but that he had all of us here. Didn't he want to stay with us? He looked at me and didn't answer. I've always remembered this moment. I think he had prepared himself to leave, and no chemo treatment was going to change that in spite of my desperate prayers for him to be healed. We can glibly say that when a loved one dies, it's God's will, but that makes God look like a bad guy. It's statements like these that are responsible for irreparably shaking up a person's faith. I'll talk more about why bad things happen in chapter nine.

You've probably wondered how, with all the millions of people sending prayers, God hears each of us. If you remember the God-spark, or Holy Spirit, or Higher Self that is in all of us, then you can easily see how God hears each of us individually. He's right under our roof. The problem is that, because we depend on our egos and have blocked out His voice, we often can't hear Him. Our job here is to break away our physical barrier, the ego, and open up our connection to our God-spark. The more we open this connection up and the more we listen, the more we hear God speaking to us. Sometimes it's just a mere whisper, sometimes a gut feeling, and sometimes it's an actual voice. I know this because I heard His voice once. It really made me sit up and take notice. I had pneumonia and was very ill with a high fever, so ill I couldn't sit or eat. I was sure I was close to death and wanted nothing to do with anyone or anything, I felt so awful. Chuck suggested I call my mother, and I just shook my head no. He was worried about leaving me alone, but all I wanted to do was sleep. When everyone had left for work and school the next day, I realized how thirsty I was but couldn't get up to get water, so I just huddled under my blanket and cried. I knew I could call my mom and she would come over, but I just didn't have the energy or will. Suddenly, a strong, male voice boomed in the bedroom, "You're shutting your mother out!" The shock of this loud voice made me bolt upright. You can bet after that moment that I called her. She came over with chicken soup.

I know that you've heard the saying that God always answers but that sometimes the answer is no when we don't want to hear it. In my experience, God has always answered my prayers, but not only does He not always answer the way I want Him to, He always answers in His own time frame as well. Infinity does not have linear time as we know it, and I think that sometimes God forgets that we're stuck in time. Thus, He sometimes seems to not be in a big hurry to let us know His response. Many years ago when we were living in Madison, I prayed for the lot next to our present home in Kirtland to become available someday so we could buy it. It was a beautiful lot to me but seemed unattainable. However, after about ten years, the farmer next door sold his land to a developer, and we were able to buy it. We still own the property. Maybe my mistake was in saying "someday."

There are different types of prayer. There are prayers of petition in which we ask for something, prayers for others when we pray for the health, happiness or safety of loved ones, and prayers of Thanksgiving in which we give thanks for all of our blessings. We recite rote or memorized prayers like the Rosary, the Our Father and the Hail Mary. We ask God to bless our food, and we express gratitude for those blessings He's brought us. He doesn't need our gratitude, but expressing it puts us in a more loving frame of mind. That's why prayers of gratitude are so important. We can also just talk to Him like we do our beloved friends and family. All of these types of prayers connect us with God and set us up to communicate with Him. In addition, prayers need to have different degrees. For the more innocent among us, prayers need to be simple, like "Now I lay me down to sleep..." for children. There are literally hundreds of prayers because there are so many different needs on the part of so many different souls. Each of us is on our own path back to God. Therefore, we each need different things. For me, for example, praying memorized prayers doesn't seem as effective as when I just go inward and begin to lay things troubling me out to God, but I still love praying the Rosary when I need to just contemplate the mysteries of God.

Prayer is connection to our God Mind, or God within us. When we pray, we raise up our vibrations to God, and God hears us, like a spider on a web that "feels" the vibrations of its prey far from where it sits. God hears all and knows before we even pray for what we think we need. When we believe and trust that we're taken care of, miracles happen and prayers are answered. We can't hear or see, though, if we don't believe.

Every religion that exists now or has existed in the past or will exist in the future is here for a reason. Religions are created at various levels of sophistication and understanding of the people for whom they exist, and each has its own rules and interpretations. The same is true for prayer. Some people require simplicity in their religion as well as in their prayer whereas others aren't satisfied with merely superficial understanding of what they are being taught. We have thousands and thousands of different prayers which have been memorized and used throughout the ages. These are very successful at bringing people closer to God spiritually.

Prayer is the most essential practice of any religion. Through metaphysical prayer, people become reawakened to God and the Spirit within us. Matthew 6:6 in the New Testament is a handbook of how to pray in a higher state of consciousness: "when thou prayest, enter into thy closet, and when thou hast shut thy door, pray to thy Father which is in secret; and thy Father which seeth in secret shall reward thee openly". Entering into your closet means to enter into a deep state of meditation. Going more and more deeply within, you will meet your God-Presence within. Jesus said that "I and the Father are one" (John 10:30), and, "I am in my Father and ye in me, and I in you" (John 14:20). By entering into a deeper state of consciousness, we can connect with God within us. It's at this point that we are truly praying.

Jesus also told us that, "…when ye pray, use not vain repetitions, as the heathen do: for they think that they shall be heard for their much speaking…" (Matthew 6:7), and He goes on to teach the disciples how to do this with the "Our Father." It's important to feel the words and think about what you're saying when you pray.

You are probably asking, "If God knows what we need before we ask, why should we even ask?" This probably does not make much sense to you, and the failure of mainstream churches to address such questions are one of the reasons why people tend to disappear from the pews on Sundays. Jesus told us that the kingdom of God is within us (Luke 17:21), and that is where we need to go to find it. We do this by meditating and awakening the God-Presence in us. If God already knows what we need, we should pray by listening first and attuning ourselves to God's Spirit within, and then by affirming and declaring thankfully that He is giving it to us. You enter into your mind, shut off your physical senses to the physical world, and enter into the inner depths of consciousness. Through this connection of Spirit with the physical realm, your prayer will naturally be in attunement with God's will. It will be answered. As you become more attuned to God's Presence, you will find your prayers are changing as well. As the conscious mind gets into contact with the Christ Mind, you will begin to bring the Christ Consciousness forward on a day to day basis. Because the infinite mind knows what we need and don't need, you will receive ABC even though you prayed for XYZ. This is why you can pray to your heart's content and still not win the lottery. Such a windfall is probably not in the chart for you, and it could cause you to stray from your original plan. This no doubt seems as if God is not answering, but in fact, He is and knows what you need. If you pray in alignment with Christ within, you won't be praying to win the lottery. When dealing with the Eternal, you will be looking at the long-term picture and how things will turn out in eternity. Your prayers will change.

If you meditate each day, you will be truly praying. The Christ Mind within will come to the forefront, and what you think will become what God thinks. This transformation is subtle but will begin to influence what you pray for. God in truth, then, will be influencing your prayer life.

The Psalmist said to "Be still, and know that I am God" (46:10). If you sit with your eyes closed and allow God to surface and give up your will to the Holy Spirit inside of you, God within will begin to work through you. You will begin to realize that what you think you need is actually God thinking through you. You are all a manifestation of God who have taken on physical bodies to learn and grow into your potentials. God is never far from you as you plough through your daily lives and difficulties. You need to remember to meet with Him, through meditation and prayer, and trust that He will carry you through your problems. When you give your will over to God, your thinking becomes God's. How can anything go wrong? You cannot make God or the Universe do anything that goes against the plan. If you are still breathing, that means that God is still within you. Real prayer works every time if you do this:

*** Meditate at least twenty minutes each day.

*** Give up your will each day to allow God to work through you. God will then do your thinking. You will interpret it as your own, but you will begin to feel that your life is being divinely guided.

When you become one with God's Mind, you will become better at what you do, doors will begin to open for you, and you will sense a difference in your perspective of life. It is a very gradual change for most people, but this change will come. Your vibration will be higher and closer to God's, and you will be better able to tune into His frequency to hear His guidance. Just remember: You are not separate from God. He is within you and always there if you ask for His help. It's up to you how close and how clearly you want to hear. Jesus said in Luke 17:21, "… for behold, the kingdom of God is within you". How do you recognize your God-Mind? You ask, meditate, pray, turn control over to God, and the knowledge will come. You will know you are growing spiritually because you will begin to experience more psychic experiences. You will have more joy, peace, calm and love in your life.

Now you might ask why, when you have prayed for a family member to come out of a coma or emerge unscathed from some horrible accident or illness, God doesn't seem to answer your prayers. Please remember that God is right there with you at all times. Accidents can be lessons on how you need to handle things and help others. Deaths are really your loved ones returning to their real homes. It's hard on you to say good-bye, but they really are returning home, and that home is a beautiful place. If you can manage to set aside your grief and believe what you have been promised, death is not the horrible event you have all come to dread and fear but rather a reawakening of your spiritual selves to the lives you left behind when you materialized. It's like the caterpillar changing into a butterfly and flying off to a better place.

This is a really hard fact to digest, so I'm leaving it here and am praying that you will begin to think all this through and begin believe in God's presence in your life. Life can really become beautiful when we lose our fears and look at the bright side of things. If you can get to the point of knowing that God is always with you, you will experience a joy and peace that you will never get from your favorite video games or Ipods. Believe me when I say that I know this for a fact.

TIP ON BEGINNING TO PRAY:

If you're not in the habit of praying and feel insecure or awkward doing so, it's really simple to start. I'll give you an example of what I say when I pray. After I meditate, my conversation with God might go something like this: Good morning, God. Thanks so much for giving us this beautiful day filled with flowers and sunshine and plenty of birds. (Obviously, this is summer. You can also thank God for the ton of snow if you live in the snow belt.) Please be with me today and guide me to do Your will. I turn my life over to your perfection and ask that you guide me where you would have me go. Please also send love and protection to my loved ones and keep them safe and happy. Help them to reconnect with You in their own time, but please be with them all. Please also take care of _____... (This is the point at which I begin to pray for others, either from my prayer chain or just those people who I think might have a need. If someone's name or face pops into my head, I'll send a prayer for that person as well.) I love you, God, and ask that you continue to teach me and guide me according to Your will. Please forgive me my shortcomings and failures and give me the strength, knowledge and will to do much better to help with your kingdom. Thank you for the blessings you've sent me. Amen.

You've asked me....

WHERE'S THE PROOF? IF SANTA AND MONSTERS AREN'T TRUE, HOW DO WE KNOW GOD EXISTS?

CHAPTER 6

Skeptics and non-believers demand proof of God's existence in their rants about there being no scientific proof. My rebuttal to this would be for them to prove that there is no God. I know that science is not at the point yet of being able to prove anything spiritual, so we have to rely on personal mystical experiences, inspired writings, and biblical and other clues handed down through the ages. While I wondered how to elaborate on this question, I grew chilled sitting in my office air conditioning and decided to venture outside into the 90-degree dog days of summer. I was experiencing writers' block anyway and needed to switch gears. When I'm blocked, I start surfing the web, checking and posting on Facebook, checking our budget and bills and just about anything else I can do to waste time when I'm trying to avoid the mental anguish of getting through a block and actually writing.

My dogs and I ventured out into the heat and seated ourselves in the shade of our huge Colorado Blue Spruce. Before long, several butterflies fluttered by, dipping in and out of my roses in their endless search for nourishment. Hearing the distinct humming of one of our hummingbirds, I watched as she hovered first over the flower buds, pecking her tiny beak in and out in search of nectar and then landing on her perch on the bird feeder while a bumble bee zigzagged near my shoulder. Birds chased one another and played tag around their feeding station. Nearby, my cherry tomatoes glowed a ripe red in the sunlight and bobbed on their vines, inviting me to pick them and sample the succulent flavor that can only be found on vine-ripened, organic tomatoes. The breeze gently rocked my wind chime and mingled its soft melody with the other summer sounds. I couldn't help but wonder just how, with all this evidence around us, anyone could NOT believe in God. Proof or not, the miracle of life is all around us. Unless a person believes in spontaneous generation and the chaos theory, this proof is clear and evident just outside our doors

If everything in nature happened just by chance, we wouldn't have the beautifully patterned monarchs and tiger butterflies and iridescent hummingbirds and wildlife that care for their young. We wouldn't, couldn't have by accident the myriad colors and scents of our summer flowers. Life and the universe would not be coordinated enough to work together to create such beauty. If it all was just chance, it would take an infinite amount of time for even one flower to come to fruition by the luck of the draw. Never mind the millions of species of plants and animals that not only are beautiful to look at but are miracles in their inner workings. Proof to me is in the patterns found everywhere we look: in the oceans, in the sky, on the ground, in the intricacies of spider webs, within animals and people, in our feelings and experiences, and in the miracle of birth. How would it be possible for an egg and sperm to meet one another at just the right moment and combine to create a human life? How does the sperm know which direction to swim? Something has created an energy for that sperm to swim so hard and so long in the right direction to find the egg and connect. Something must direct the cells from that union to begin dividing and differentiating into the correct organ and tissue cells to create a tiny human being. It must be much more than just attraction and repulsion. There is an intelligence behind all of nature, and that intelligence is God. Scientists have learned much about life and have, in fact, been successful in cloning many animals, but they still fail to explain what force is behind getting life to begin to grow. Just observing nature, then, is one way to gather proof of God's existence.

When I teach research methods to my college students, I explain about triangulation. This means that if several sources begin to state the same facts or information, the students can assume that it's factual. Obviously, they still need to vet the source, but when three or more sources say the same thing, it is probably reliable. This is another method of pointing to the proof of God's existence. Thousands of Christian mystics, philosophers, and saints have talked of beatific visions of Heaven and God's glory and have related personal revelations of contact with God. Saint Bernadette, Bernadette Soubirous, was one of the first mystics that I read about as a child, and her story transfixed me. She was born to a prosperous family which, through unfortunate circumstances, lost their means of support and became quite poor, living in a one-room cell which had once been a prison cell. In 1858, at the age of 14, Bernadette had her first vision of a beautiful lady dressed in white with a yellow rose on each foot. When she told her parents of her vision, they told her not to return to the cave, but she was drawn back and disobeyed their wishes. She was cruelly interrogated by authorities who questioned her sanity, but she was still compelled to return to the spot where she had a total of eighteen more visions. On one visit, the lady asked her to drink from the spring. Seeing no spring, Bernadette began to dig in the mud and returned home covered with filth. Several days later, water began to flow from the spot at which she had dug, and people began to experience miraculous healings from that water. Today, Lourdes is a major attraction in France. Bernadette was posthumously canonized by the church. Her body, which was exhumed, is said to be perfectly preserved. If God is not real, many people must be pegged as liars in this case, including Bernadette and all those who have been healed by the spring at Lourdes.

So many mystics through the ages have provided us with "evidence" of God's reality that it would be impossible to list all of them. St. Therese of Lisieux, "Little Flower," interceded for many and supposedly brought miraculous cures to the ailing. She wrote about her experiences in her book, *The Story of a Soul.* Joan of Arc heard "voices" and led the French army to triumph over the English as a result. Saint Padre Pio had multiple mystical experiences, as did Saint Anthony of Padua, and the hundreds of mystics and seers since have all pointed to irrefutable evidence that God does, in fact, exist. One of my first connections with a modern-day mystic was a biography of Edgar Cayce, *There is a River: The Story of Edgar Cayce* by Thomas Sugrue, and this book started me on my journey in Metaphysics.

Early on my spiritual path, I was awestruck by the writings of psychics Jeanne Dixon and Ruth Montgomery. Dixon wrote *A Gift of Prophecy,* and Ruth Montgomery documented revelations of the other side of the veil. Both authors propelled me further on my quest for knowledge of the spiritual realm. Unfortunately, just as in many walks of life, there are fakes and charlatans who claim they're mystics. You need to choose wisely in following or believing anyone. Follow your instinct, and never give up thinking for yourself. If someone is coming from any position besides love and is making you feel guilty, afraid, angry or judgmental, run as fast as you can. There are people who peg themselves as spiritual leaders who would deprive you of your family, finances, love and support in the name of God. A great deal of harm has come about as a result. People in so-called "churches" have been led to commit mass suicide or murder, so you must always be vigilant of the "wolf in sheep's clothing." Your spiritual journey is your responsibility and no one else's. Don't give away your own power.

If you're familiar with the Bible, you must know all the stories of Jesus's miracles. He walked on water, raised the dead, cured people, fed people, turned water into wine, and on and on. These are not just fairy stories but actually happened. I believe them because I have also experienced miracles in my life, albeit much less dramatic than those attributed to Jesus. I prefer to call them mystical experiences, although some have most definitely been miraculous.

I've related the many times I've prayed and manifested what I prayed for. I previously described the mystical experience I had when I was a teenager and at Mass with my grandparents. I saw a beautiful, golden orb over the altar that filled the church with a golden light. I was overwhelmed with love and an almost orgasmic joy that stayed with me long after the Mass had ended. At the time, I had no idea what orbs were, so I just believed it was a sign God sent me to let me know He was there with me. I know that today people have theories about orbs ranging from dust on camera lenses to angelic beings to ghosts to schizophrenia. I follow my gut and my feelings since that's how God communicates to me. An overpowering feeling of love and joy could not come from anyone else but God. What I saw was definitely spiritual and began to change my life, moving me forward on my spiritual path.

I've had other mystical experiences since then. Once in deep meditation, my soul moved up and out of my head, and I felt the most incredible expansion into the universe. It was an actual physical feeling of expansion out of my body, and I floated with the stars. I've had several "initiations" on the other side of the veil as well. One spectacular incident was another expansion into the universe during a psychic dream. My entire physical body blew up like a balloon and floated into the universe. I was filled with such all-encompassing love that the feeling remained with me for weeks afterwards. Psychic dreams are different from regular dreams. They are crystal clear, filled with joy and love and you don't forget them whereas regular dreams fade quickly. I've smelled aromas from loved ones who have passed and heard voices from the other side. One particular aroma I've been experiencing lately has been Old Spice, the fragrance that my father used to wear all the time. I'm convinced he's near. During a Mass intention for my mother who recently passed, I smelled her White Diamonds perfume. During this past Easter Vigil, I experienced a miracle during Mass. When my priest was holding up the cup and wafer, the wafer was red with a golden aura surrounding it. I kept blinking to clear my eyes, thinking I was seeing things, but the red remained. After Mass, I mentioned it to a fellow choir member who excitedly exclaimed that she had seen it, too. This was an unexplainable miracle, but a miracle nevertheless.

I've experienced healing miracles in my life as well, and these events have further proven to me beyond any doubt that God is real and exists. Many years ago at a conference, I was involved in a session in which a leader led us in a group meditation exercise to demonstrate the psychic abilities we all have. Holding hands, we hummed "omm" together and then did a short meditation. The members of my group of ten were strangers to me, and I had no idea what their professions were. During this meditation, I felt a surge of energy moving through me. We completed our exercise and continued with the rest of the conference until it was time to return home. During the drive home, I suddenly realized that my sprained wrist which was in a splint had been healed. Someone in the group had channeled enough energy to heal me. This energy comes from God.

I recently discovered with a broken heart that my little Maltese,

Crystal, has heart disease like her mother. She's twelve, and I had hoped to have more time with her. One morning, she went into congestive heart failure. I took her to our vet, and he very apologetically told me she had very little time and that he could do nothing more for her. I cried and cuddled her that entire day as she struggled for breath. I called the vet again the next morning thinking he would suggest putting her down. Instead, he told me to give her a couple more days to see if she rallied. She was lying on the back of our couch gasping for breath and breaking my heart, so I prayed. As soon as I asked for help, I felt calmer, stopped crying and pulled up a chair to channel Reiki through my little baby. Normally, she runs away when I try to channel Reiki energy to her, but she was too weak to do anything and just lay there very still, struggling for each breath. I really felt the energy flowing through me and into her. After about twenty minutes, her breathing became normal. I continued for another twenty minutes and wrapped her in a blanket to sleep quietly on the couch. Her brother climbed up next to her as if protecting his little sister, and she slept through the day and night, only arising to relieve herself. The next day, she was much perkier, and eventually, after about a week, she acted almost normal with the exception of the heart disease cough. I don't know how much longer we have with her, but I've been thanking God ever since for the reprieve. I channeled the energy, but it came from God.

Another miracle we witnessed as more proof of God's existence was with Chuck's Uncle Sam. He underwent surgery for his emphysema but didn't survive the week. The day after his passing, a flower that had been on his beside and hadn't bloomed for a while opened. Although this was not a sign I personally witnessed, knowledge of it is further proof of our existence on the other side.

God's plan is beautiful. If you open your eyes, you'll see his majesty everywhere. When you become too immersed in technology, you fail to really "see" the miracles of life and the signs God sends to encourage and comfort you. The "death" of everything in the winter miraculously returns to life in the spring and parallels our own journeys of birth, life, transition and birth into spirit. These are clear signs of an extreme intelligence guiding and building our universe. Someone or something on the quantum level powers up life. It can't just be spontaneous generation or universes could be created in petri dishes.

Non-believers call God a crutch and a myth. Everyone strays, including the most devoutly spiritual people, and I can't think of a better crutch than our God. Calling for His help surpasses using drugs, alcohol or tobacco, and there is no after-effect. He also doesn't damage our health.

Is He a myth? Many myths come from truth. Maybe even unicorns were once alive, but that's a topic for another book. Some people debate the merits of parents "lying" to their children about the reality of Santa Clause, but I've never thought it was a lie. Saint Nicholas was a real person who went around helping children. The story has it that he threw gold coins into the window of some daughters who were going to be sold into prostitution, thus saving them from this horror. The church canonized him, and his spirit lives on the other side of the veil and also in the personification of Santa. Although the myth is exaggerated, we can say that he really existed and that he is still alive on the other side. His spirit affects us most profoundly during the Christmas season and the winter equinox when the veil to the other side is thinner. We feel his spirit of love and giving and demonstrate this spirit especially during the holiday season.

Writers write what they know. Stories of good versus evil, mythological dragons, unicorns, all are embedded in our subconscious minds, and myths told in many different places from different times all have certain similarities. No one can say how much truth our myths hold. Stories of God, miracles, angels and guardians are too numerous and too similar across our various religions to just pass them off as total fiction. Within the pages of the Bible, the Koran, Kabbala, and ancient and modern literature, the truths found in all of our sources verify to me the fact that we were all created from one God. All these signs point to yes, there is a God.

MEDITATION AND PRAYER TIP:

Sit in your safe place, close your eyes and relax from your toes to your head, breathing deeply in and out. Clear your mind of all thoughts. When they invade your consciousness, push them out. Breathe in and out three times deeply, and ask God to be with you as you open yourself up to Him. Visualize a golden orb just above your head, and then see it slowly move down, covering you completely. Imagine it is outside you as well as permeating inside and filling you with an all-encompassing love and warmth. Continue for as long as you're able, and then, with your picture of God in your mind, just start talking to Him as if He's right there. Ask Him to open up your eyes so you can see clearly. If you have anything you feel badly about, bring that to Him to take care of. Thank Him for all you've received and, with a grateful heart, ask Him to bless you and your loved ones. If you want to begin to find God as a personal God for you, ask Him to begin to send you what you're ready for. If you have others who need prayers, tell God about them and ask that He envelop them with His love and healing. Sit quietly for as long as you need and contemplate your image of God. End with an "amen" and "so it is." Believe that He's heard your prayers and is answering.

You've asked me....

WHY DO WE HAVE TO GO TO CHURCH ON SUNDAY? WHAT'S THE BIG DEAL?

CHAPTER 7

Do you remember me telling you how thoughts are things and so to try to guard what you think? Have you heard the saying that bad things come in threes? There's a reason for this, and the saying has truth to it.

Life can be challenging in this physical world. You're far removed from your spiritual homes, and as you venture out into the world, it's easy to become enmeshed in mundane things. You awaken in the morning to a new day, get ready to go to school or work, and might happen to turn on the morning news, where you hear of "...wars and rumours of wars..."(Matthew 24:6). You're suddenly bombarded with news of terrorist acts and murder and people committing atrocious acts against one another. You're told that people are losing jobs and starving, the stock market is about to crash, and global warming is threatening your very existence. Feel-good stories about people helping others, if there are any, are reserved for the very end of the news and are not deemed worthy enough for the ratings, so you often miss out on these small crumbs of goodness. Even if you don't begin your day with the news, you are still showered with negativity and gloom and doom.

It's easy for your thoughts to plummet, pulling you down with them. Where your thoughts go, so go your lives, believe it or not, and it's an easy jump into the pit of negativity. Sending out negativity draws it to you, and this is why people often observe that bad things happen in threes. For this reason, it's wise to break away from the daily doldrums and become immersed in spirituality for at least one day. What better day to do that than Sunday, our "day of rest." Church attendance can refresh you and prepare you to face another grueling week of the same challenges. It helps to break that cycle of negativity so you can start the next week fresh.

When you were little, your dad and I made it a point to attend church every Sunday for this very reason. It helped to "center" us for the day and, hopefully, the week as well. It was an activity we did as a family. Sunday church is an opportunity to rest, rejuvenate, and spend time with family and friends. We tried to set the day aside for church in the morning and then often went to Grandma's home for a pancake breakfast. This helped create a strong sense of family in your world. Even to this day, you're close to your cousins. Sunday dinners were equally important to me to provide my family, and we tried to make them peaceful, conversational times during which we could all touch base. I still believe that gathering round a dinner table is important when kids are growing up. Starting with church on Sundays at least helped me feel complete and away from the chaos of our working lives during the week.

Jesus told us that "...where two or three are gathered together in my name, there am I in the midst of them" (Matthew 18:20). This is another perfect reason for church attendance. The power of prayer is amazing and can work miracles when many people congregate to hear God's message. You may have been told that hypocrites attend church and then go forth and sin over and over, or that people fill the churches only on holidays and take space away from the "regulars." My perspective, however, is that something is pulling that person to attend church. Attending once a year is better than never attending, and at least people try. Something draws millions of people to church or their places of worship each week. It's that God-spark that's in all of us that's subtly tugging that person to move toward God.

"Church" doesn't necessarily imply a building. God's "church" is where people are gathered worshipfully. It can be on a hill or in a garage or in the slums of Paris. Where "two or three are gathered together...," God is there as well. Miracles have occurred in such places. One miracle happened in April, 1968, a time when I was excitedly planning for my graduation from high school and a subsequent trip to France. I regret having been oblivious about its occurrence at the time. Millions of people saw an apparition of the Virgin Mary hovering over a church in Zeitoun, Cairo, Egypt. The apparition lasted a period of four years, and Christians, Muslims, Jews, Catholics, Protestants and non-believers all witnessed it. Hundreds of publications reported it with photos. One reputable source was *The New York Times*. If you google the title, "Visions of Virgin Reported in Cairo: Coptic Bishop among those who tell of Apparition," you can read the article on May 5, 1968, on page 71. Many sick were cured, the blind received sight, and there was an incredible renewal of faith in God and the world of spirit accompanied by a mass repentance.

Miracles happen in church. Remember the vision of the golden orb as well as the blood-red communion wafer that a fellow choir member and I saw on the Easter Vigil of this year? One of the main reasons for Catholics to attend church is to partake in the Eucharist. I've grappled with an explanation of the Eucharist for a long time but have finally realized that I'm going to have to wait for the answers to how some things happen. Sometimes science just can't explain things.

Because we attended protestant churches for about twenty years, the mysticism of the Eucharist was lost on me for many years. After I returned to the Catholic Church fifteen years ago, I was stumped to discover the Catholic belief that the bread and wine were, in fact, the real body and blood of Christ. To the protestants, it's symbolic, but not to Catholics. It's the real thing to Catholics, and try as I might, my studies in metaphysics and all the meditating in the world didn't explain this mystery. As children, you're told how to believe, and you do, until you grow up and are told not to believe. "Except ye be converted and become as little children, ye shall not enter into the kingdom of heaven" (Matthew 18:3). To "enter" or become conscious of Heaven, you must believe like a child does. The modern rational person who thinks through logic often doesn't believe in miracles, and, especially in this computer age, you are hard-pressed to see the miraculous in anything. Church is one place that still talks about miracles.

You've all had your doubts, and priests are no different. A priest in eighth century Italy had his doubts as well about the reality of the Eucharist. During Mass one day, as he was saying the words of consecration, "This is my body…this is my blood…" he looked down and discovered the bread had turned into real flesh and the blood had transformed into five globules of blood. This relic has been on display for over a thousand years, not preserved but not deteriorated either. In 1971, an Italian professor of anatomy conducted scientific tests on both and found the flesh to be actual heart muscle. The blood tested as if it was fresh blood (*The Eucharist*).

Another doubting German priest in 1263 who was traveling on a pilgrimage to Italy also had questions about the Eucharist being Christ's actual body and blood. During Mass, he suddenly realized that blood was dripping onto the altar cloth. He stopped Mass and took the cloth to Pope Urban IV, who preserved it as a miraculous relic. It supposedly is at the Cathedral of Orvieto today.

Moving to more modern times, a priest in 1996 discovered an abandoned wafer on the floor and immediately picked it up and placed it in water. A blood-like substance grew. In 1999, Dr. Robert Lawrence of the United States examined it and determined it to have human DNA with active living white cells. Science and even metaphysics don't answer the how or why of these events (*The Eucharist*). We can only accept them believing, like a child, without logic and reason.

When Jesus took the bread at the last supper and said, "Take, eat; this is my body..." (Matthew 26:26) and "Drink ye all of it; For this is my blood of the new testament, which is shed for many for the remission of sins..." (Matthew 26: 27, 28), He wasn't kidding. It really is His body and blood, and for now, at least, science has no explanation. Miracles happen in church. You're taught to believe in Jesus's miracles of walking on water, turning water into wine and healing illnesses. Jesus knew even back in his lifetime that his disciples would find it difficult to believe in the Eucharist, and throughout the ages, He has left us with clues to His truth. He gave us the gift of His living self through the Eucharist and fulfilled His promise of being with us always. This concept is troubling for many, and non-believers have even gone so far as to call it cannibalism. For those who believe either through faith or by witnessing something miraculous, each Host we consume and wine that we drink fills us with His love and energy. We know He is always living and always present with us and in us. Jesus came to open up a new consciousness that's heart-based instead of ego-based and died for our sins. He took upon himself our "sins," or disconnect from God, to help us to awaken to who we are and to reconnect with our Father. We thus go to church to share in His living body, blood and love as food for our souls and to help with this reconnection.

Church attendance also helps you to immerse yourselves in God's glory. If you remember what I explained in previous chapters about vibrations, the significance of the statement, "…when two or three are gathered together in my name, there am I in the midst of them" (Matthew 18:20) shows the importance of being in church. Many people worshipping God together automatically raise their vibrations, sending up waves of energy into the different kingdoms described earlier. "Love conquers all" is a universal truth. When evil is met with love vibes, it runs like the devil and cannot win. When entire congregations get together to pray, mountains can be moved, storms can pass, and people can be healed. I've seen this on our prayer chain time and again. Nothing is more powerful than when many people gather to pray for the good of all.

How important is it, then, to attend church? The Catholic Church teaches that it's a sin not to go. If the definition of "sin" means distance from God, that's true. If you don't attend, you certainly will not be tossed into the burning fires of hell, but you will probably not be as connected to God as if you attended regularly. This disconnect can become your own private hell. People have told me that they don't need church to be spiritual, and that is absolutely true, but church certainly helps to center people once a week and helps you to better withstand the stressors of life. Church attendance also helps you to learn about your particular religion and spirituality if it's a true church and not interested in power and control. Because going to church helps people to connect to and focus on God, church attendance can accomplish much good for the human race. You shouldn't go simply because you fear going to hell if you don't go, nor should you go simply out of a sense of obligation. Rather, you should go because you love to connect to God and to others of like mind where you can pray together and address problems together and build a better world together. Seeing how Pope Francis brought so many millions of people together during his visit to the United States supports this. For the week he was here, the news covered his loving acts and talks, and people pulled together, at least for that brief period of time. We have yet to discover the effects of his visit, but I'm certain they'll be long-term. Together, in the spirit of love, people can accomplish so much more than if alone, and attending a church of your choice makes this easier. We can strengthen our country and the world, we can build schools and hospitals. We can run orphanages and give hope to people by following the words and deeds of Jesus's teachings. The church helps to keep us focused on doing these good things.

I recently had the privilege of helping with the collection and assembly of food baskets to be taken to people in need in our community. People from our church family showed up in droves to help out. People coming together to help others happens all the time, and that help is spearheaded in the churches. People want to help, and the church provides the venue to do so.

Attending church helps you to get motivated to work as God wants you to, to recharge you to do His will. Worshipping as a family helps you to take small steps toward peace in your families. This peace leads to small steps toward peace in your church and communities and in turn leads to small steps toward peace in the world. Larger and stronger military and weapons will not achieve this peace, nor will it offset evil, hatred and fear-mongering. Interfaith dialogues and getting to know all people who are not like you will. All true religions teach and spread love and peace and bring people together from all walks of life. The goal should be to build a tolerant, inclusive society and world that's free of injustice for anyone. You can be a catalyst for good by attending a truly spiritual church.

MEDITATION AND PRAYER FOR PEACE

When I'm really troubled and in need of a soothing prayer and meditation period, I do the following: (note: this takes approximately an hour to complete, so allow yourself enough time so you don't worry about the clock.)

Go to your quiet place and do your rhythmic breathing as explained in previous chapters. When you're centered, ask God and the angels to wrap you in a white protective light. State that you wish to do God's will and align yourself with His will. You'll do seven groups of seven breaths, visualizing with each group of breaths a different chakra clearing out blackness. For example, for the first set of seven breaths, breathe in and out quickly seven times while visualizing your base chakra spinning a clear red. For each subsequent group of seven breaths, do the same as you move up your chakras. Visualize each chakra spinning clear and bright. Following this breathing exercise, chant "Om" three times, pronouncing it like "Ahhm," which is calling God's name. I then pray the rosary, but you can choose any prayer meditation that you find peaceful and helpful for you. Prayer beads help. After this, for a half hour, allow yourself to go into a deep, peaceful meditation. Focus on the area of the third eye and try to keep errant thoughts from invading. Coming back to the present, pray. Thank God for your blessings, ask for healing for yourself and others, and ask for God's peace for you, your family, the country and the world. Just talk quietly and naturally with God. I close this with the *Our Father* and the *Glory Be*. This prayer and meditation session has gotten me through some of the worst times of my life.

You've asked me....

HOW DOES GOD TALK TO US?

CHAPTER 8

My priest delivered a homily one morning on how God talks to us and told us that one of our parishioners who was facing a grave decision had come to him to ask how to tell whether or not it's God talking. He told her that just having the question meant that God was communicating. Another time, a young seminarian, Maxwell, came to speak at Mass one morning and described how he had discerned his call to the priesthood. One night, Maxwell had dreamt of his guardian angel telling him that, if he prays, he will hear God. He knew this was a true vision because of the clarity of the dream compared to other typical ones. He began to pray, and God led him to the priesthood. God sends synchronicities and messages coded in text passages received at just the right time along with signs. He speaks to us through scripture, visions, miracles, music, and teachers appearing exactly when we need them. Our intuition and feelings are God trying to get through to us. Occasionally, He even speaks to us in a regular voice, as He did to me when I was very ill. He uses all of these methods to communicate. Because we are so accustomed to hearing and seeing all of these messages, we tend to disregard them as coming from God and miss many of them.

One of the most important means God speaks to you is through your feelings and intuition. When you're just beginning to realize that

God, in fact, is always with you, answering your questions and prayers, it can be difficult to discern His voice. There is so much noise today in society with I-phones and tvs and radios blaring that you hear more from others and the media than you hear from God. It's easy, then, to mistake that "still small voice within" for your own imaginings. How, then, can you really tell it's God speaking to you? It's simple. The Bible guides you: "Go within," you're told. How many times do you remember me telling you to follow your gut instinct and things will work out? That's because that's the main way God talks to you: through your instincts and intuition. Remember the stone wall I was on when I received an overpowering feeling to get down just as my friend Agnès came to push me off? That was God or His messenger saving me from destruction.

Another time when I was in high school, my best friend Sally and I were driving in our 1964 booger green Mustang convertible, enjoying a balmy summer night and just cruising around Kirtland. Before all of the developments on Garfield road had sprung up, it was dark and desolate. I turned down it to see where we would end up. Suddenly, we both had an overpowering fear of something that happened so simultaneously for both of us that I turned around and went back to Mentor. Neither of us had a clue as to why we had both become scared at the same time, but we listened. Who knows what would have met us at the end of this dark road. Listening to God through my feelings has saved me from potentially harmful relationships with men, as well. I listened to my gut when everyone else was telling me not to marry my man. A beautiful marriage that's lasted 45 years has proven I was absolutely correct in listening to God rather than to my friends and family.

In order to listen, the first thing you need to do is clear your minds and thoughts of everything that troubles or worries you and ask God for guidance or help, whichever you need at the time. Jesus told you,

"Ask, and it shall be given you" (Matthew 7:7). How many of you have actually asked? There may be lots of reasons for not having asked. Churches have laid on the guilt feelings to make you feel selfish and self-centered if you ask. You seem to believe that you need to figure things out for yourselves. Parents have even perpetuated this myth. God loves you as you are, and He has not sent you into this world alone and poorly equipped to handle your struggles. The reason you have taken on a physical body is to learn how to become what you were meant to be: Gods. Yes, Gods, and as His kids, he hasn't left you alone to figure it out yourselves. Once He helps you, though, you need to act on His advice and not sit back and sleep.

Many churches teach that you're sinners and have sinned from the grave on. For this reason, you should forever beat yourselves up. This is one of the most enormous mistakes I believe that churches universally have made. How can babies be sinners and not worthy of God's love? Impossible. We are children of God. What parent doesn't love his or her children even though they make mistakes while learning? If it's true that parents love their kids, it's an insanity that God does not. We can pretty much accept the reality that God does love us and that perhaps church and society and sometimes even our families who have judged us as being unworthy are wrong. Period.

The next thought, then, is that, if God loves you and you have nothing to be ashamed of, how do you know things? If God and Jesus are always with you, how do you know this, and how do you tap into their help and guidance? This might take a little practice and work, but the effort is well worth it and will reap great rewards. It will make God happy as well. The majority of people believe that God is a philosophy or an abstraction and not really available for personal help. You learn about Him your entire lives and may or may not believe in Him, but not too many of you really place Him in the position of a loving friend or parent who is always at your beck and call whenever you need advice, help or simply companionship. You're told to trust in God, but when the chips are down, it can be hard to trust in someone you can't see or feel, but He's right by you. You're just not listening. I'm sure you've heard many times how God loves you and talks to you, but if you haven't been aware of His direct communication, this becomes a platitude to file away with the rest of the church teachings that sound good but really don't seem to work in your daily life. If you just know how to pay attention and listen, you will really begin to "hear" Him.

So, how do you begin to listen to your heavenly parent? The first thing you need to do is to ask for knowledge. I did this many years ago when I was in my early twenties, and it has been a life-long journey to the answers. As I have said, I know I'll never know it all, but I certainly never get tired of finding the truths God sends me.

After I asked initially, books and people began to appear in my path. I could tell I was ready for what came because of the feeling of excitement I received when they appeared. They were always exactly what I needed at the time. You can go on-line and find many titles that will help you start. I also began to meditate, which is listening to God. In order to receive answers, you need to fine-tune your vibrations so you can pick up what He is telling you. I've learned over the years that, because it's such a natural thing to hear God's voice, you may have been hearing it all along and simply have thought it was your own voice or thoughts.

How do we tell the difference between God's voice and our own? Going back to the answer in the Bible, we can tell by the fruits your thoughts bring. If the actions make you feel joy and love, you're on the right path and can be assured that it's God's voice. If the action helps others or yourselves, it's coming from God. All of you have experienced such thoughts, but many times you've ignored them. Try this. Go into a meditation: close your eyes, focus your inner sight onto the middle of your forehead, and try to maintain that focus while keeping out your thoughts. Sit quietly and think about connecting to God. This takes practice because your minds are so active, but you will get better at it as you practice. If you really want to begin to open yourself up to listening to God, you will need to do this every day. Doing it at the same time of day is preferable. You will probably only be able to do this for a few minutes to begin, but eventually you will go into an altered state of consciousness and be able to remain there for longer and longer periods of time. You'll know if you're falling asleep because your head will begin to nod. Pay attention to what transpires within. You may begin to see clouds of purple, and you might even have flashes of pictures inside your head. These are indicators that you're raising your vibrations. As you do this, you'll become more and more attuned to God's voice.

God also talks to you through prayer, or at least, He listens and then talks to you when you meditate. From the time I was a child, I've had many spiritual experiences, and I value each one. As I said earlier, in elementary school and later, I was able to pray to find things, and they would appear. I did this a lot as a child, but as an adult, it has also worked for me. During one phase of our lives when we were pretty broke, Chuck was working as a fireman and had to get contacts for his mask. He promptly lost one in the bathroom. This was a volunteer job, and he had paid a fortune for these contacts since contacts were an extravagance at this time. I was upset because I didn't know how we were going to be able to afford another pair, so we combed the white-tiled bathroom floor where he had lost it. It was nowhere to be found. I sat down, cleared my mind of thoughts and emotions, and had a chat with God. I told Him nothing He didn't already know since He knows what we need before we even ask, and I asked Him to help us find this contact. I finished, went into the bathroom, and there was the contact in the middle of the floor. Since it was tinted brown and our tile was white, there was no way it had been there previously. I'm beginning to have senior moments at my age now, and I often lose things. You can bet I still call on God to find lost items.

When things have looked really bleak financially, I've prayed for help, and we have always received what we needed. To illustrate one such incident, we needed twenty dollars that we didn't have. I prayed, and then I found a twenty dollar bill in our yard. More recently, we were really strapped since I had quit my job and needed money to meet our financial obligations and to catch up. I prayed for what we needed, and that month, all that we needed came to us, some of it through refunds, some through realizing we had an account we didn't know about, and some just within our budget when some bills weren't as high as I had thought. The fact is, we received what we needed that month. The same thing happened a couple of months later as well.

Jesus told you that "if you have faith the size of a mustard seed, you will say to this mountain, 'Move from here to there,' and it will move. Nothing will be impossible for you" (Matthew 17:20). This means something, and how many times have you heard it? However, you haven't trusted it. When you're confronted with something very scary, it's difficult to place your faith in God, particularly if you haven't been talking to Him prior to the difficulty. If, however, you take this statement to heart, set aside your own egos, and trust that what Jesus said was the truth, you'll be amazed at what changes occur in your lives. Try it. Ask for help and keep your senses open for the answer.

I'll admit that sometimes I don't practice what I'm preaching here and am still learning this lesson of trusting in God. We had a very lean summer not too long ago, and on a particularly horrible day, I was slammed with some very large and unexpected bills, one from an insurance screw-up. I hate dealing with insurance companies, so when this happened, I of course sat on the couch and just cried. After having a very good cry and letting it all out, I tried to go into a meditation and then prayed for help and guidance. I told God that He had told us to give all over to Him, so I asked Him to please deal with the insurance company for me along with the other creditors. The next day, I felt a little better but only because I kept reminding myself to trust in God and not to worry. It was hard, but I did it. That day, I got a call from the insurance company telling me that it had been their error and that they were taking care of it. I was also able to pay the other unexpected bills because the college called and asked me to teach an additional class that quarter. God certainly stuck to His promise and took care of the situation.

God talks to you all the time on a daily basis, but you shut Him out. I don't think it's intentional. You've been taught by churches, schools, and society that God is not real, and you have to depend on yourselves. You go to church and are taught to believe in God, but then people will scoff if you tell someone there that "God told me this or that." An actual true faith and belief are not really there, even for those people who attend church each and every week and never miss. If you're attending church and repeating the Statement of Faith and are participating in the rituals, why, then, do you think, "Yeah, right!" when someone says he can hear God talking? This doesn't make sense to me, and it's puzzling because I've been talking to God all my life. Hiding this fact gets old, and it has taken a long time for me not to be fearful of admitting to my communication.

God is our Father. Most fathers talk to you. You need to listen so you can hear, and that's the only roadblock. Priests and ministers are not the only ones privy to this communication. You all can listen and hear and talk to God, but most of you have been programmed to shut out this idea of actually talking with God. Persecution toward people who admit to mystical experiences has gone on for a long time. The early church tortured, and the inquisition brutalized mystics, witches, and people who they thought were a threat to the church. You've been taught that you're sinners who are not deserving of such a benevolent God. Sinners, according to some, are not worthy of direct communication and must go through an intermediary. How silly.

God gave you free-will and, as God's child, if you choose incorrectly because of that free-will, it will cause consequences that perhaps will bring suffering. This should teach you not to make such a poor choice again. The consequences should keep you from doing it. You're not being punished because of the consequences. Rather, the universal law of cause and effect works its magic to teach you, and that's another way God uses to talk to you. God is not going to throw you into the flames of hell because of a poor choice. He still loves you and still wants a relationship with you. The more you learn, the better choices you make and the closer you can feel you are toward God. He doesn't stop communicating with you because you are a "lowly sinner." More often than not, the communication block is from you. You have moved away from Him and can't hear His voice.

We have all heard God in different ways. God has spoken to me in visions, feelings, dreams, "coincidences" which are not really coincidences, actual clear pictures I see in the back of my eyelids, and I've heard His voice. Everyone has had these and more but just didn't know them for what they were. As an intuitive, God speaks to me through my feelings more than anything else. There have been times when I just felt in my gut to pick up the phone and call someone, and it turned out that that person needed to talk. This happened with a friend who was having problems. She just needed to talk at exactly the time I called. Another time, I had a dream that was crystal clear and pictured a friend I had not seen in a long time. Her hair was a mess and thin, and she was crying. That morning I called her and discovered she had been battling cancer. She told me my call really helped. I'll never forget the time I actually heard His booming voice telling me to call my mom.

Once I was at a crossroads and needed help making a decision. For some reason, I couldn't decide what to do. I asked God to send me a sign that I was aligned with what He wanted for me. Looking up, a clear image of an angel appeared in the clouds. This was tangible and not an obscure, questionable or arguable sign.

I previously described my vision in church when I was in high school, and I know it was God or Mary or Someone Divine. It was a golden orb, and I felt the most incredible peace and love. I don't know the reason why I had this vision other than to simply reassure me of God's Presence, but when I'm having a rough time, if I go back to this vision, it calms me.

Prayer works. When Hurricane Patricia was predicted to hit landfall in Mexico with over 220 mile-an-hour winds, the call went out for everyone to pray. I helped, and many prayed. This massive hurricane dissipated before it hit Mexico. I talk to God constantly throughout the day, not just in prayer but conversationally. He created us for companionship, after all, and I feel connected most of the time. That doesn't mean I don't get scared or worried about things, but I am working now on turning over all my worries to Him to work out, so this is what I talk about. I also ask for advice on what to do and listen for answers which come in various ways: hunches, ideas, thoughts, or pictures behind my eyelids. Different people will experience differing modes of hearing God's voice. Some people will receive smells or physical sensations, some see actual pictures all the time, and others will have the gut feelings. I've had all of them. God has bombarded me with ideas to put in this book. I have to be sure to have pen and paper handy because many times the ideas come when I'm in the shower. If I don't write them down immediately, they quickly fade away.

You need to develop the means you have of hearing God through daily meditation, asking, and then trusting that God will be there for you as Jesus promised. It's a life-long adventure to this knowing, and that, in fact, is one of the reasons you are here: to learn how to do this. I'll admit I'm still a work in progress in giving all my worries over to God and letting Him handle things.

MEDITATION:

Face east toward the sunrise, stretch and sit in a relaxed posture. Breathe in and out deeply, clearing your lungs after each breath, and for a few minutes, just sit and focus on your breath for as long as you can. Remain relaxed, and make certain your muscles aren't tensing up. Think about God's majesty and all He's created. Think about who He is and ask for a closer relationship with Him. After several minutes, thank God for giving you another glorious day, for your family and friends, for your job and home, for enough food to eat and for whatever else you're thankful for. Thank Jesus for His sacrifice for all of us, thank the angels and saints for their help, or just sit quietly feeling grateful. Ask Him to show you the secrets of the universe. If you need help with any problems, ask Him to help, whether it's for help with a decision or for money to pay for something or for someone's return to health. Remember, though, that what you ask for for someone else might not be their path, and it might appear as if God doesn't answer when you ask to cure someone. We don't know when it's someone's time to go. Only God does, so don't let that divert you from believing in God's answer. I'll end with the Lord's Prayer, the Glory to God and Hail Mary prayer, and close. Saying "Amen" produces the sound of all of the names of God over the ages, and it also means, "And so it is." This is how I choose to end my prayer and meditation sessions. Remember, "Ask, and ye shall receive...", so I ask.

You've asked me....

IF THERE IS A GOD, WHY DOES HE ALLOW HORRIBLE THINGS TO HAPPEN?

CHAPTER 9

On a rainy September morning, we awaken to yet another Breaking News report stating that a young boy is in the hospital fighting for his life following a school shooting. On the same day, we hear of a disastrous train wreck that killed one innocent bystander and wounded up to 100 other people. Russia is showing aggression and hacking our computer systems, North Korea is testing nuclear weapons, and Isis seems to be spreading everywhere like a deadly virus. Negativity explodes at us from all of the news channels as reporters scramble to focus on murders, shootings, bombings, terrorism, accidents, and just about every other bad thing that can possibly go wrong in our world. Any person, even the most devout and faithful, is bound to wonder why God seems to have no control over our world. Believe it or not, however, God is alive and well in spite of the chaos we see in our lives. The world is working as it should be. God's hand is with us, but we are the culprits causing all the chaos and destruction.

We all have a purpose for being on this planet, and that is to learn, to grow, and to become more spiritually enlightened so we can evolve back to God and keep Him company and do His work. Life is way more complicated than just being born, growing up and then dying. The whole process displays the genius and beauty of God's Creation. It takes more than a lifetime to evolve into what we're supposed to be, so God has given us the opportunity to experience a multitude of lives, growing and hurting and experiencing joy in each one. Whether we are fast or slow learners depends on us and determines how quickly we reach enlightenment. So far, Jesus is the only one who has gotten there, but we all eventually will, too. He even tells us so in John 14:12: "Verily, verily, I say unto you, he that believeth on me, the works that I do shall he do also; and greater works than these shall he do."

As new souls, we slow down our vibes to materialize and enter this earth plane and learn what we need to learn, gravitating to the life and lessons that we need for our spiritual growth. Our lives are like a wheel. We get on it and, through involution, move down and then up until our lives culminate in final oneness with God. Think of a glop of mud on a huge wheel. As the wheel turns, it starts changing shape while the wheel goes down. At the very bottom, it's squished into a hardly recognizable form. Then, the wheel begins to turn upwards, and the mud splatter takes on an even different form. At the top, the splatter achieves perfection. Involution is downward progress, and evolution is upward. We come into materiality on the physical plane many times and move on this wheel until our spirit bodies are developed enough to return and remain whence we came. On this journey, we experience things, make many mistakes, learn, and grow. In this process, we can create lots of trouble and cause bad things to happen. God allows this so we can mature into perfected beings. I can remember in school passing along some gossip and hurting one of my friends. Later on, someone I had thought was a friend did the same thing to me. I experienced that same hurt that I had caused my first friend. It was a tough lesson, but

I learned from it and now try not to pass on lies about anyone. The devil didn't make me do it. I did it all by myself. Like everyone else, I still have a long way to go to be a better person. Real evil is caused by people's actions.

With each progression through our different lives, our spirit bodies begin to grow and develop. When in the physical, our ego is the center of our being. The Ego is our "I", or self, and the mediator between our physical reality and us. It's our conscious self that controls our thoughts and behaviors and connects us to the physical world, keeping us alive. Through our perception, our ego controls our feelings and emotions and is very self-centered out of necessity to keep us alive. As we progress and grow spiritually, however, we begin to sense more and more of the spiritual world and move more to a heart-centered awareness that operates out of love rather than self-preservation. As our spiritual/psychic senses become more developed, we develop a greater awareness of the world of spirit. Some people take longer than others, and their growth can be slowed or stopped, as in a Hitler or a serial killer. Eventually, we all make it back. Through our ego and our need for self-protection, we experience greed, pride, selfishness, arrogance, hatred, and fear. Because of our distance from God, which is our "sin," we're afraid. We fear going hungry. We fear aggression. We fear not having enough of anything: love, food, property, money. All of these feelings then sprout, spread and can cause deadly destruction in our world. Violence, crime, war, selfishness, and murders become a part of our lives . This is the devil, personified to represent our egos.

We can opt to speed up our spiritual growth. My late father-in-law told me once that he didn't know if there's a God, but if there is, and when he meets up with Him, he has some serious questions to ask. It's hard to see bad things happen to good people. Why do kids have to suffer with horrible diseases? Why do loving parents die early, leaving their bereaved children behind? Why do these things happen if there's a God? We've all asked these questions at some point in our lives because one of the most painful things to see is suffering, especially a child. By choosing to incarnate in a defective body or by having children with serious illnesses or crippling defects, we can make much quicker progress because of the challenges of the situation and the love that grows from it. We decide this on a soul level, and this choice helps us to grow more quickly spiritually, even though we can't see this growth at the time. In every bad thing, like a child getting cancer, something good comes out of it and serves as a lesson in our spiritual growth, even if we can't see it at the time. Perhaps money is raised for research, or a doctor discovers a cure or new treatment. We might realize how strong we can be for others, or maybe we just need to experience the tragedy. There might be a karmic lesson for the afflicted person. Life's lessons are hard, and this school is tough, but to become what we are becoming, we need the tough lessons. We often need to look hard for that silver lining, but it's there somewhere.

Bad things can happen because of the choices we make. We're free to choose and either choose through our ego or our heart. Our Earth school uses dualities to reinforce our lessons. We don't know light without darkness, good without the bad, rich without poor, happy without sad, or right without wrong. By experiencing duality, we are able to find unity in the presence of both, and this knowledge creates change that moves us from the ego's "me-centered" perception of reality to a more heart-centered perception. If not for dualities, we would have no idea what works and what doesn't. We wouldn't know cold if we didn't experience hot. If we had no war, we wouldn't value peace. With no pain, we wouldn't know comfort. When I was two or three, I went around our house with a bobby pin, putting it into all the cracks and crevices. When I found an outlet, you can be sure I learned about electricity when I zapped the entire house and myself. Matt learned about red-hot burners the hard way as well. This is how we learn, and the lessons are tough. As free spirits with freedom of choice granted to us by God, we choose our paths, our lives, our beliefs, and even our parents before "falling" into materiality. Once we're here, we learn through our choices, and sometimes these choices cause bad things to happen to us. The dualities we come across help us to see the differences and make better choices either in this life or our next.

Since our choices are often those we make from ego-based perception, one tool the universe has provided to teach us is the law of Karma. Newton's third law of motion states that for every action, there's an equal and opposite reaction. This law applies to the physical world but is also active in the spiritual realm. I've clearly seen karma in interactions in my teaching job. A great example surfaced during a teacher's strike, when our board president hurled horrible insults directed toward teachers. She used her power as a board member to bounce people out of their jobs and replace them with her cronies. Karma reared its head, however, when she lost her job and experienced the same things that she had subjected to some of our teachers. I've observed over and over again someone being ugly to another person and then experiencing the same thing, usually more profoundly than the first person had dished out. This works positively as well as negatively. I remember one time running into a car while it was parked, and I left a note on the door offering to pay for the damages. Nothing came of it, but years later, when I was attending our local urban college where the crime rate was high, I came from class and saw in the parking lot that someone had slammed into my rear fender but had left a note with insurance information on it. This is the message in the movie, *Pay it Forward*. What goes around, comes around, and this is what the Old Testament is referring to in Leviticus 24:19, 20 in the King

James Bible: "And if a man cause a blemish in his neighbor; as he hath done, so shall it be done to him; Breach for breach, eye for eye, tooth for tooth: as he hath caused a blemish in a man, so shall it be done to him again." Jesus also talks about karma when he says, "Put up again thy sword into his place: for all they that take the sword shall perish with the sword" (Matthew 26:52). The movie *Pay it Forward* illustrates the law of Karma perfectly. When something bad happens, it's not the devil or God's judgment or punishment. Instead, it's the law of Karma balancing things.

People, then, cause evil, but God has it all under control. He gave us our lives as mini-gods, or His children, and as any good and loving Father, He didn't just dump us here and disappear. When He sent us to this earth-school, he wove a veil in our consciousness to make us forget where we came from so we wouldn't be trying to constantly come home. He also created in us a fear of death so we would try to stay alive as much as possible along with pain to tell us when something is very wrong. If you look up the etymology of the word sin, the Hebrew root means to miss or to forget. Somewhere through the ages we've been taught that we're all bad and not worthy of God's love because we have sinned from birth. I've mulled that over and over and have never been able to figure out how a brand new baby can be a sinner before the world even begins to impact him or her. When my research led to this definition, I rejoiced. We're all sinners, YES, but that's because it means we have gotten distant from God, not because we're bad. It's because the very act of "falling" into materiality creates distance from God and disconnects us from His love. Early churches have emphasized our badness to help keep us under control through the fear of going to hell. As children of God, we can't be bad any more than our kids are bad since we all have His spirit within us. We just make bad choices that cause consequences.

But, you say, the Bible tells us all about sin. The devil is the leader causing us to fall into his grasp. He's the cause all of our problems, people tell us. Paul says in Romans 6:23 that "...the wages of sin is death...," and we've been taught that, if we sin, we die. News flash: we ALL die. No one gets out of this life alive. We come into the physical and then have to return by shedding our physical bodies. Our sin is our separation from God. Jesus came to help bring us back to living heart-centered lives and to remember our origin. You might ask how it was that Adam supposedly brought forth the first sin which mankind has been repaying ever since, as Paul says in Romans 5:12: "...as by one man sin entered into the world, and death by sin; and so death passed upon all men, for that all have sinned..." A quick course in numerology can explain how Adam represents mankind and isn't just one person. Vowels are omitted, so the Hebrew and Greek letters ADM for the name Adam have numerical values of 1, 4 and 40 respectively. If you reduce this by adding these numbers together, they total 9, which is the number which represents humanity. 9 also represents the number of our present evolution, but that's another story for another book. Further evidence of 9 representing mankind can be found in Revelation 13:18: "Here is wisdom. Let him that hath understanding count the number of the beast: ***for it is the number of a man***; and his number is six hundred threescore and six." Reduce this the same way, and your sum is once again 9, denoting mankind. Interestingly, man is formed after nine months of gestation, and we have nine orifices: two eyes, two ears, two nostrils, one mouth, and two lower extremities.

According to Revelation 14:1, "A Lamb (Jesus?) stood on the Mount Zion, and with him an 144,000, having his Father's name written in their foreheads." The number of people who will be saved is 144,000. If you add these together, you get 1+4+4= 9 again, the number of humanity and the number of people saved. It's all of us! We still have a lot of work to do to grow and become enlightened, but it might make some of you feel better to know you're not destined to burn in hell's furnaces because of some wrong you may have done. It also means the neighborhood bully that's been harassing you is destined to be saved, as are felons, addicts, Hitler, and everyone. No one is better than anyone else, and this knowledge really levels the playing field.

So who is satan, then? We're warned constantly of the evil that is lurking nearby to tempt us into doing bad things and that he's alive and well in this world. Watching the news would tend to support this belief. As stated in Revelation, we all have heard that the sign of the beast is 666. Again, add the numbers 6+6+6, and you get 18. Add 1+8, and you get 9: the NUMBER OF MANKIND! MANKIND is Satan if we block God's spirit within us, and WE are the ones who cause the wars and murders and terrible things that are happening. MANKIND caused the Holocaust through thinking one group of people is superior over others. MANKIND caused the inquisition in the name of the church. WE have caused the corruption and nastiness we see every day in the news. We cause this through our ego's perception of some lack which creates fear. This fear leads to a need to control which creates a struggle for power and greed. Then, our actions coincide with these nasty perceptions, and evil flourishes. The devil doesn't make anyone do it. It's our own egos operating through self-preservation and blocking love, which is the most powerful force of energy in the universe. The number of the Beast which holds us back is 666: humanity. The story of Lucifer falling from God's grace is symbolic of the story of us falling into materiality. Our own egos are the tempter.

God, then, doesn't allow bad things to happen. He allows us to live our experiences. By allowing us our freedom, bad things happen because of us. We get to take the responsibility, and we all are responsible. We've experienced the Holocaust and learned about inhumanity and the effects of a lack of love. We've experienced many shootings and are learning about the pain of bigotry. Bad things can create good. World Wars I and II brought great changes and new technologies to the world. Jet engines, radar, medical advances and computers all came from the war effort. Learning of the horrors of concentration camps has helped us to see the effects of man's inhumanity to man. We cannot hide behind the phrase, "The devil made me do it," or "the deceiver is waiting to make us stray from our path." We are the ones who can do either good or bad in our world.

One horror that I have not yet mentioned is the horror of watching our loved ones die. All of us have prayed to spare those we love from their fate. When they die anyway, it feels as if God either isn't there or is and doesn't care enough to allow them to live. Most if not all of us have lost people to cancer. I prayed for my dad to get well. He didn't. Our physical bodies become ill for many reasons. It might be karmic in nature, it might be a reaction to the way we've treated our bodies through our lives, or we might have, on a soul level, agreed to meet a certain fate to help someone else learn a spiritual lesson. Many years ago, I read an excerpt from a medium who had channeled a little boy who had passed from this life and was contacting his mom years later. His death had caused her to begin to search for God. As a result, she learned a great deal about spirituality and grew toward enlightenment. He told her in the channeling session that he had agreed to live a short life so she could learn this lesson. Tough love, but she grew spiritually. It's no consolation when a loved one is dying, but it's helpful to remember that as the physical body deteriorates, the dying process releases a newer, more shining version of the soul who had entered this life as a new baby. The actual moment of death is, in fact, the new birth of that soul into the higher planes. I've been at the sides of several people as they passed, and it's a very gentle, peaceful process. People on the other side are there to welcome the person back, and the person ready to pass on often reaches out to those folks. We cry for our loss of them in our lives, but they aren't dead. They are probably more alive than we are here on this earth plane of existence.

Knowing about life beyond physical death helps those left behind. During the last four weeks of her life, my mother said that, when she passes over, she was going to get my dad, my brother, my uncle and my aunt, and they were all going to come and get her sister. Aunt Bea had Alzheimer's and had been in a vegetative state for many years. Two days after my mother passed, my aunt left this world. Mom meant what she had said and had come and gotten her sister. Knowing that they are all together again brings me peace.

Obviously, I do not believe in any hell other than our own distance from God. Jesus told us specifically how to get into Heaven when He said, "Love the Lord thy God with all thy heart, and with all thy soul... and thy neighbor as thyself" (Luke 10:27). This love is the energy that permeates our universe and world and connects us to God. When we all begin to turn from our ego-based actions and live more heart-centered lives connected to God's love, we'll begin to see real change in our world. It's all up to us with God's help.

MEDITATION DURING THE LOSS OF A LOVED ONE:

If you're at the bedside of a loved one who is in the throes of passing on, it's crucial that you re-energize yourself and prevent a plunge into despair, both for yourself and for your loved one. This is a meditation that I use in this case:

Lie flat or sit in a comfortable position and breathe in and out several times, deeply. Clear your mind of worries or grief if you can, and focus on a place or event that you shared with your loved one that was happy or enjoyable. Continue to let your mind remember the good times you had with this person, focusing on their good health and your comradery. If your mind wanders back to the present emotional challenges, bring it back to the happy place, and try to remain there for several minutes or as long as possible. Begin to visualize what your picture of Heaven is, and see your loved one walking into that place, happy and healthy and in their vigorous body that you knew before. Continue with visualizing them doing whatever made them happy in this life until you grow tired or feel ready to quit. End with a brief prayer for their relief from their suffering and gratitude for their participation in your life. Take some deep breaths, and you can end the session. This has helped me and, hopefully, will help you with your grief.

You've asked me....

HOW DO YOU SOLVE THE CONFLICT BETWEEN SCIENCE AND SPIRITUALITY?

CHAPTER 10

Imagine a society that burns all books. You might love reading histories, but because they offend someone out there, they're banned. If you're caught with them, firemen burn them and then imprison you. You might love to read spy thrillers, but the government has deemed these dangerous to national security, and they're banned as well. Because every book has the potential to offend someone, all books are made illegal. This is the society that Guy Montag experiences in Ray Bradbury's *Fahrenheit 451,* and if we're not careful, we could be in the same boat. Religious extremists constantly battle rigid scientists who can only visualize what they can prove through scientific method. The two opposite viewpoints cannot seem to meet. The loser in this battle is all of us when the war between science and spirituality reaches the courts and it becomes illegal to teach one or the other viewpoints. This is crazy since the *Bible* and science do not conflict but rather explain one another.

Advocates for teaching Creationism believe that the earth is very young and was created in seven days while evolutionists maintain Earth was created over eons of time and is at least 4.5 billion years old. The *Bible* can and should be read on a variety of levels and does not contradict scientific theories. An explanation for how the world began is explained in Genesis 1, and science explains more factually how it may have occurred. The two explanations work together.

Genesis 1 describes the formation of the universe in seven days. The theory of evolution demonstrates how this was done. Moses states that "the earth was without form, and void; and darkness was upon the face of the deep" (verse 2). Before the Big Bang, according to theory, there was nothing. Just a void. This void was not empty but was filled with the spirit of God, which is His consciousness. Moses describes this when he refers to the "face of the waters." God said, "Let there be light: and there was light" (Gen. 1:3). There was nothing at this time but spirit, but when God spoke, there was light. God's voice consists of vibrations. According to NASA, the second after the universe was formed, the heat and vibration created matter. Couldn't it be possible that God's voice, or vibrations, set the Big Bang theory into motion? This was the first day of creation, and it took eons and eons. This first day refers to the first level of the world being created. At first, everything was dark, but as free electrons floating around began to meet up with neutrons, they started to form atoms, and this allowed light. Something needed to start this reaction. This force could have been no other than God. Science has failed to explain what got everything moving, but Genesis does.

With God's spirit still pervading everything, different spiritual levels of the earth began to split and form. Again in Genesis 1, God said, "Let there be a firmament in the midst of the waters, and let it divide the waters from the waters..." (verse 6). The definition of a firmament is sky, so God "said," or sent vibrations, to divide the waters from the waters. Jesus refers to "rivers of living water" (John 7:37-39) metaphorically as the Holy Spirit, or the Spirit of God. This is the spirit that was present before the formation of the universe and to which Genesis is referring when Moses mentions the "waters." When he talks about the division of the "waters from the waters," Moses means that God's energy is moving and forming molecules to define the different levels of existence. Scientists state that the atmosphere was too heavy and toxic to sustain life at this time. Genesis states "God made the firmament, and divided the waters which were under the firmament from the waters which were above the firmament...and God called the firmament Heaven" (verses 7, 8). This could be the separation of the world of Divine Spirit from the world of Virgin spirits. Again, this took eons, not just one day, although this was described in the Bible as the second day.

I'm no Earth scientist, so I really can't precisely describe how the earth formed, but I do know that heat played a role in forming land. Genesis describes the third day of God's creation as that time in which the earth formed, and plants and animals appeared. If you research earth history, you can read about the different epochs of earth development millions of years ago. General science classes teach us that some fossil discoveries support the early life forms that began to inhabit the planet. Scientists have described the different time periods which fit in beautifully with the third day of creation described in the book of Genesis. Over a period of millions of years, life began to appear in the form of minerals, plants and cellular animals. The plants produced oxygen which helped to prepare the earth to sustain more advanced life forms. Life began to evolve.

The fourth day in the book of Genesis concerns the formation of the sun and the moon to separate the days and nights and provide the seasons. This is a description of the further development of the planets in our solar system. The fifth day follows, bringing forth the animals, and on day six, man is created. Scientists place early man's appearance much more recently on this scale at about 2.5 million years ago. Although the Bible describes the entire creation as being completed in seven days, this is metaphorical and denotes the creation of the seven different spiritual worlds. This does not contradict science. Instead, it's illogical to think that all of this could have happened in just a week. Genesis 2:4 says, after this "week" of creating, "These are the generations of the heavens and of the earth when they were created." The word "generations" refers to multiple years, not just seven days. Although this analysis is very unscientific, it makes a good case for teaching and learning both creationism and evolution.

Science and spirituality do not conflict. Even Pope Francis has said that Big Bang and evolution do not conflict with the Bible and that God is not a magician. God uses natural laws of Physics, Chemistry, Mathematics, and even Logic in His creations. The universe is not chaotic but is logical in its workings. The creation of the universe could not have happened without an intelligent force starting the process. One law God uses and which is described in Genesis 1 is the law of Biogenesis, which, according to Webster, is the theory that "living organisms come only from other similar living organisms" (Webster, p. 148). God commanded, "Let the earth bring forth grass, the herb yielding seed, and the fruit tree yielding fruit after his kind, whose seed is in itself" (Genesis 1:11). He states further in verse 24, "...Let the earth bring forth the living creature after his kind, cattle and creeping thing, and beast of the earth after his kind...", illustrating the law of Biogenesis. Jeremiah 33:25 and 26 affirms that God states that He himself follows natural laws: "If my covenant be not with day and night, and if I have not appointed the ordinances of heaven and earth; then I will cast away the seed of Jacob..." Natural laws have created a logical and orderly universe. This creation would not have been possible by chance.

The law of chemistry is the most obvious natural law that God used to form the universe but is also the most difficult for me to explain since I am no chemist. Very simply, the universe is made up of electrons, protons and neutrons which vibrate. Through the laws of attraction, repulsion, adhesion and cohesion, they group together in atoms to form elements. If these atoms just bounced around haphazardly, we wouldn't be able to logically place them onto a periodic table, nor would they accidentally morph into various forms of matter. If such a coincidence was possible, scientists would be able to create universes in petri dishes. This is proof that someone had to be behind it all.

The Bible describes what God did, but science explains how He did it. In creating man, God needed some means of doing so, and science can explain that means in the theory of evolution. Just observing nature and looking around, we know that evolution is a reality and that minerals, plants and animals cannot simply pop into being. Just as the universe is formed, so is man. As the Hermetic axiom states, "As above, so below," God formed man in a parallel manner to His formation of the universe. The first world He created was the world of pure, God or Divine spirit. God resides here. He next formed the world of individual spirits which were us as sparks. In this world, we knew no differentiation from God. As God began to think of form, the world of thought and the idea of form began to take shape. Within this world came mind forms, or our beginnings as individuals. He created the desire and etheric worlds and then the physical, and as our spirit began to crystallize into matter, our consciousness began to develop and reside first in mineral forms, then plants, animals, and humans. This describes evolution. This theory, again, runs parallel to the Creation story and does not contradict anything. God's tool to create man was evolution. As man's consciousness grew, the need for a more sophisticated vehicle grew as well, and over millions of years, we see different types of humans evolving. It could very well be that once upon a time, we were all trees and resided in different life forms to learn and to grow. I love the book, *The Once and Future King,* by T.H. White because it describes Wart's experiences living as a fish, a hawk and a badger in order to learn the lessons of humanity. Perhaps we've all gone through the same type of experiences and have evolved past the need to use these vehicles.

As I've said previously, agnostics and atheists proudly proclaim that those of us who are spiritual must need God as a crutch, and that's why religions were created. If that's true, I can't think of a better "crutch" to use than God. The people who make such statements have, sadly, never experienced any type of miracle or mystical experience. Science can't explain everything. In fact, I'm not sure science will ever be able to prove God's existence, but those of us who know God personally don't need that proof. We see it every day in the miracle of sunrises and sunsets, the death of nature in the fall and its rebirth in the spring, watching animals and insects who know instinctively how to live and mate and survive, and receiving physical answers to prayers. When I ask for help and a sign that God hears me and I see a distinct angel in the clouds, or I pray for help to find something and it materializes, my assurance that God is real is reinforced.

The non-believer or the person who has spent no time in trying to get to know God misses out on some of the most exciting and joyful experiences of life: that of experiencing first-hand what God can do. I still have difficulty explaining the Eucharist, but the miracle I experienced on Easter proved to me that, even though I can't explain it, it happened and was real. I've had so many mystical experiences that I have no doubt about the existence of God and the spiritual world. One day in celebration of our 45th anniversary, Chuck and I visited the fountain of Lourdes in Euclid. I had a broken foot so, while he hiked the grounds, I sat in front of the fountain that ran over a rock from

Lourdes in France and went into a really deep meditation. I immediately saw purple clouds that formed into a silhouette of Mary, and I was filled with a glorious feeling of peace and love. Usually, if I'm in a strange place with people walking around, I find it difficult to meditate, but the vibes here were so spiritual that I was easily able to do so. All of the signs of the reality of God and a spiritual world are there. We just need to be aware so we can see them.

Today's society makes it difficult to experience and hear God. People are glued to their phones, tablets and computers every second that they can be, and they're plugged in during any leisure time. Instead of developing their own intelligence and intuition, our young people rely on technology to do their thinking and research, and any gut feeling that might come from God is buried. Shows like the *Bachelor* perpetuate the myth that we can't find the right partner without going through a logical process of evaluating candidates. When I was in the dating scene, I knew the person I clicked with and had a connection to without having to march them through tests. IBM is developing a new artificial intelligence computer that the company claims can access all the data out there on a particular subject, form a hypothesis and make a better analysis or diagnosis of the problem than a person can. They maintain that this computer digitizes creativity. This is frightening. It seems that we're giving away our humanity and our connection to God and relying more on the technology we invent. The more we rely on these gadgets, the more we will be cutting off the communication from God, and the more convinced we will become that God is not there. Fear, strife, hatred and turmoil will take over as we experience greater and greater distance from God. We will be the ones that moved away, not God. The danger is that all that makes us human, our compassion, character, love and God's spirit within us, will be shunned in favor of the machine. We all need to continue in our Search for God to prevent this.

FINAL MEDITATION:

I've tried to keep my own church out of this since I'm writing about spirituality and not about Catholicism, but I want to describe how I pray and meditate in case any of you might want to try it. It takes about an hour but balances my chakras and helps me to get into a deep meditation and prayer session from which I usually emerge refreshed and ready to tackle the world. It works for me, and maybe it will for you as well. I've described much of this meditation/prayer period previously.

Sitting in a comfortable position, I take in three deep breaths and focus on relaxing all of my muscles from the toes up to the crown of the head. I ask God to surround me with protection in the thought of the Christ, and ask that my very breath, my going in and coming out, will be in accord with God's will. Visualizing each of the colors of my chakras, then, I breathe in and out seven times. For example, as I visualize a clear red spinning ball of energy at my root chakra, I breathe in and out seven times. I move to my sacral chakra and visualize a glowing, orange ball of energy spinning clear and sparkling and breathe in and out seven times. I move up to my solar plexus chakra and visualize a clear yellow spinning ball and breathe seven times, and then do the same at my heart chakra, seeing a shining emerald green ball of energy. I visualize my throat chakra as a brilliant blue, and then my third eye chakra spinning a clear indigo. Finally, I visualize my crown chakra as deep purple, spinning clear, and do the seven breaths as I move to each chakra.

I then sit for a moment and clear my mind, focusing on God's spirit descending on me and moving from my crown chakra to my feet and back up. I try to feel the energy while staying relaxed. At this point, then, I pray the Rosary, and this is the Catholic part of my prayer and meditation session. When I've finished this, I usually am in a pretty deep meditation state and remain that way until I feel it's time to return to reality. I then pray for family, friends and people that need it or whose names pop into my mind, including our world and church leaders, and I send out love into the universe. I end by asking for help if I need it and close with "Amen, and so it is." This really works for me and sets a beautiful tone for the remainder of the day.

CONCLUSION

God is real. He is not just a cliché that you hear about in your church or from your parents. He is not meant to be feared in any way. He wants our companionship and wants to help us in this life of ours. He can be found in our churches, synagogues and mosques, but He is also in our homes, our gardens, our schools, and even our prisons. He loves us like we love our children and pets and then some, and He is not going to throw us into a blazing furnace when we exercise the free will He gave us to make bad decisions. Our free will and choice, our egos, are the true devils of the world, the satan depicted in the Bible and folklore. When we distance ourselves from God by not loving and connecting to our life source, we are in hell.

God created a beautiful universe. When we sin, or do things that disconnect us from God, we are unable to experience the glory of our world. We start to think negatively. We become fearful and then begin to turn on one another. This is the cause of neighbors feuding as well as world wars, and the politicians will not be able to stop the viciousness until we stop it, one individual at a time. We can do this by getting to know and trust God. When we are truly and consciously connected, we can only love everyone and everything. All else in the world will fall into place. Can you imagine such a universe? "The Lion and the Lamb shall lie together." It can happen but must start with our full knowledge of God and His Creation.

So, to sum up what I have been writing about:

1. Everyone is equal to everyone else. Rich people are not better than prisoners, kings are not better than subjects, and teachers are not better than students. There should not be any tiers or strata of higher ups and down-unders, and no one should feel inferior to anyone.
2. There is no hell or devil who made us do it other than what we, ourselves, create and then have to live with.
3. We are NOT evil sinners who should grovel in shame in the mud. We are simply children (of God!) who sometimes, in our ignorance, make poor choices and then have to suffer through the consequences of those choices. As children, we are NOT inherently evil, and God does not punish us. The Law of Consequences does the job.
4. God is on EVERYONE'S side, whether a person is a Muslim, a Jew, a Christian, or even an atheist. We all have that spark of God within us, and we all are loved by Him. I'm certain that some of our actions probably disappoint or hurt Him, but His love is forever and unequivocal. This includes wars. For anyone to say that God is on our side and against the other demonstrates a lack of knowledge of what God is all about.
5. Life goes on and on and on and on forever. It's not over just because our physical casing has died.
6. In light of all of this, what do we really have to be afraid of?

Love,
Jill, Mom, Grandma, Mrs. B.

WORKS CITED

Holy Bible. Authorized King James Version. Zondervan: Grand Rapids, Michigan, 1994.

The Eucharist. "In Communion with Me." Love and Mercy Publications, nd. DVD.

Webster's New World Dictionary of the English Language. The World Publishing Company: New York, 1968.

Printed in the United States
By Bookmasters